Solving Your Company's Corporate Governance Issues

Financial Times Management Briefings are happy to receive proposals from individuals who have expertise in the field of management education.

If you would like to discuss your ideas further, please contact Andrew Mould, Commissioning Editor.

Tel: 0171 447 2210
Fax: 0171 240 5771
e-mail: andrew.mould@ftmanagement.com

MANAGEMENT BRIEFINGS
GENERAL MANAGEMENT

Solving Your Company's Corporate Governance Issues

ANDREW CLARKE

**FINANCIAL TIMES
MANAGEMENT**

FINANCIAL TIMES
MANAGEMENT
LONDON · SAN FRANCISCO
KUALA LUMPUR · JOHANNESBURG

*Financial Times Management delivers the knowledge,
skills and understanding that enable students,
managers and organisations to achieve their ambitions,
whatever their needs, wherever they are.*

London Office:
128 Long Acre, London WC2E 9AN
Tel: +44 (0)171 447 2000
Fax: +44 (0)171 240 5771
Website: www.ftmanagement.com

A Division of Financial Times Professional Limited

First published in Great Britain 1999

© Andrew Clarke 1999

The right of Andrew Clarke to be identified as author
of this work has been asserted by him in accordance
with the Copyright, Designs, and Patents Act 1988.

ISBN 0 273 63719 3

British Library Cataloguing in Publication Data
A CIP catalogue record for this book can be obtained from the British Library.

All rights reserved; no part of this publication may be reproduced, stored
in a retrieval system, or transmitted in any form or by any means, electronic,
mechanical, photocopying, recording, or otherwise without either the prior
written permission of the Publishers or a licence permitting restricted copying
in the United Kingdom issued by the Copyright Licensing Agency Ltd,
90 Tottenham Court Road, London W1P 0LP. This book may not be lent,
resold, hired out or otherwise disposed of by way of trade in any form
of binding or cover other than that in which it is published, without the
prior consent of the Publishers.

10 9 8 7 6 5 4 3 2 1

Typeset by Boyd Elliott Typesetting
Printed and bound in Great Britain

The Publishers' policy is to use paper manufactured from sustainable forests.

About the author

Andrew Clarke (LLM Bristol University) is a qualified solicitor who has 5 years' practice experience and extensive teaching and training experience at University level. He has been in charge of the Business Law and Practice course on the Legal Practice Course (LPC) at the University of the West of England, Bristol since 1991. (This course has consistently been rated as 'excellent' by the Law Society and is regarded as a leader in the market place.)

He has published in the business law field and is the author of *Business Entities: A practical guide* published by Sweet and Maxwell, London, 1996.

Contents

Acknowledgements   xii

1   Introduction   1
    The aims of this book   3
    The main parts of this book   3
    Getting value out of this book   5

2   UK corporate governance: scene setting   7
    Overview   9
    What is corporate governance?   9
    The origins of UK corporate governance: the 1980s   11
    The 1990s: 'kinder, gentler'   14
    What are the main corporate governance models?   16
    The UK corporate governance 'business efficient' model   17
    Questions and answers: overview of corporate governance issues   18
    Why take corporate governance seriously?   19

3   The corporate governance jigsaw: pieces, players and issues   21
    Overview   23
    The key UK corporate governance issues   24
    The corporate governance pieces   24
    The Cadbury Report 1992   24
    The Greenbury Report 1995   26
    The Hampel Report 1998   27
    The key players   28
    Questions and answers: pieces, players and issues   29
    Themes of the UK corporate governance emerging model   32

4   Corporate governance for the board: general issues   35
    Overview   37
    The director's role in the company   37
    The board's role   37
    Distinguishing management from governance   38
    The management–governance spectrum   38

	The board's 'specific' role and 'context' role	39
	The board and the stakeholders	41
	The directors' legal position	43
	The board's role in corporate governance	44
	Applicability of corporate governance for listed and non-listed companies	45
	Corporate governance issues summary for the board	46
	Corporate governance issues for the board *vis-à-vis* a specific director	49
	Non-executive directors	52
	Compliance strategies for the board	54
	Boardroom template for corporate governance	56
5	**Particular board issues: non-executive directors**	**59**
	Overview	61
	The general role of the non-executive directors in relation to board functions	61
	Non-executives and board sub-committees	62
	The importance of the independence of non-executive directors	64
	The key indicators of independence of the non-executives	64
	Overplaying the monitoring role	66
	Independence and compliance statements	66
	Non-executives and smaller companies	67
	Non-executive directors' template	67
6	**Particular board issues: the sub-committees on directors' appointments, pay and the audit**	**69**
	Overview	71
	The nomination of directors' committee	71
	The remuneration committee	73
	The audit committee	75
	Template for the board sub-committees	76
7	**Particular board issues: internal control**	**77**
	Overview	79
	General points as to internal control	79
	Risk management	80
	Template for internal control	80

8 Particular board issues: compliance statements — 83

Overview — 85
The scope of compliance statements — 86
Compliance and the Cadbury *Code of Best Practice* — 86
Types of Cadbury compliance statements — 86
The Greenbury Report and compliance — 87
The Hampel Report and compliance — 89
Compliance strategies for the board — 90
Compliance statements template — 91

9 Particular board issues: ethics and ethical codes — 93

Background — 95
Defining ethics — 95
Formalising ethics — 95
The content of ethical codes — 96
Making ethics work — 97
Ethics template — 97

10 Corporate governance for the company's auditors: general issues — 99

The auditor's role in the company — 101
The auditor's legal position — 101
The role of the auditors in the corporate governance matrix — 104
Auditors and their external review function — 107
Auditors getting it wrong: their legal position — 107
Corporate governance issues to watch out for: auditors — 109
Auditors' template — 110

11 Financial issues: operating and financial review (OFR) — 111

Background — 113
OFR in the USA — 113
The practical ramifications of OFR — 114
Content of the OFR — 115
Reviews — 116
Particular risks to be identified in OFR — 117
OFR template — 117

12 Financial issues: going concern — 119
Background — 121
The going concern statement — 122
The content of going concern statements — 123
Going concern template — 123

13 Financial issues: interim reporting — 125
Background — 127
Stock Exchange requirements as to interim reporting — 127
Current issues — 128
The Cadbury Report and interim reporting — 128
Compulsory interim reporting standards — 129
Interim reporting template — 130

14 Corporate governance for the shareholders — 131
An overview — 133
The shareholder's legal position generally — 133
The importance of 'shareholder returns' — 135
The role of the shareholders in the corporate governance matrix — 135
The role of institutional shareholders in corporate governance — 138
Shareholders' template — 142

15 Corporate governance for the company's employees — 145
The employee's role in the company — 147
The employee's legal position — 147
The role of the employees in the UK corporate governance matrix — 148
The Asian corporate model: employees first — 149
Employee template — 150

16 Corporate governance and the company's regulators — 151
Identifying a company's regulators — 153
Formal regulation — 153
Informal regulation — 154
Environmental concerns — 155
The corporate governance matrix — 157
The emerging corporate governance matrix in tabular form — 157

17 UK corporate governance: emerging and future trends — 159

Corporate governance: its changing nature in the 1990s — 161
Changing economic models — 163
Year 2000 corporate governance — 165
Other year 2000 issues — 167
Identifying key facets of the UK corporate governance approach — 169
Headline corporate governance issues — 170
The UK and refining the corporate governance model — 170
The emerging corporate governance matrix — 171

18 Two corporate governance case studies — 173

Overview of the case studies and the approach taken — 175
Corporate governance scenarios — 176
Case Study 1: Old Tower PLC – boardroom indiscretion — 177
Case Study 2: Johnson PLC – director's pay — 184

Glossary of terms — 191

Bibliography — 197

Acknowledgements

I wish to thank Professor Alan Bensted, the Dean of the Law Faculty and Dr Adrian Chandler, Director of Resources and Deputy Dean at the University of the West of England for their provision of research time, and Associate Professor Ian Campbell, Dean of the Faculty of Law at the University of Western Australia.

I would also like to thank Kevin Stewart and Philip Pullinger of the Australian law firm, Messrs Pullinger Stewart, based in Perth, for their support and encouragement in the completion of this project and the members of the Mackrell International Legal Group of firms.

I should also like to thank Dr Stella Swain for her unstinting support, and Ariana Potts and Deanna Bondi for their very efficient assistance in finalising the manuscript.

Finally I would like to thank Andrew Mould, Commissioning Editor at FT and the rest of the editorial team for their friendly and efficient efforts in seeing this project through to completion.

1

Introduction

The aims of this book   3

The main parts of this book   3

Getting value out of this book   5

The aims of this book

As the name of this book *Solving Your Company's Corporate Governance Issues* (which we will simply refer to as *SCG*) suggests, it is designed to be solution based and practically oriented.

'Corporate governance' has become something of a sprawling growth industry in the 1990s. There are several reports to focus on, and an increasing number of publications in the area, many of which go into great detail or focus on esoteric and philosophical issues connected with corporate governance.

SCG aims to provide you with a 'quick handle' on corporate governance; a ready-reckoner, as it were, to the ballooning field of corporate governance. It acts as a basic roadmap to the area; it provides you and your management team with:

(a) a starting point on corporate governance issue identity and strategy;

(b) 'warning signals' as to when your business may have a corporate governance problem; in this sense it is aimed at being an 'early warning device' for you and your fellow management team, recognising that timing is critical in dealing with corporate governance issues;

(c) the broad-based strategies on offer to you and your business to effectively counter the corporate governance issue or problem; and

(d) a guide to the sort of issues you and the management team may need to get help with from the business's professional advisers including its lawyers, accountants, auditors, public relations strategists and so on.

The main parts of this book

SCG can be read in a straight narrative format, i.e. chapter by chapter in a logical sequence or, alternatively, it can be used such that you can dip in and out of the text and go to specific issues and topics. There is a comprehensive index at the back of *SCG* to assist you in this purpose. As to the format of the main sections of *SCG*, the book is divided into 'introductory and overview issues', the 'substantive chapters' and the 'case studies'.

The introductory and overview chapters

These essentially are:

- Chapter 2 (general matters);
- Chapter 3 (key players, documents and issues in terms of corporate governance);
- Chapter 17 (contemporary and future corporate governance issues); and
- Chapter 18 (two case studies).

Chapter 1 aims to provide you with a broad-based overview of the key contemporary corporate governance issues. Some of the issues discussed in Chapter 1 are picked up again and expanded in Chapter 17, so that *SCG* comes 'full circle', as it were, in terms of current and future corporate governance trends.

The substantive chapters: 3 to 8 inclusive

The chapters themselves are designed to take you through the issues in as logical a format as the wealth of diverse corporate governance issues allows. Hence the corporate governance issues affecting the board of directors, which are, in effect, the linchpin of effective corporate governance strategy and implementation, form the basis of the first 'substantive' chapter (Chapter 3). The chapter dealing with directors and corporate governance comes ahead of the chapters dealing with the other corporate governance stakeholders, such as shareholders and employees.

The case studies

The case studies in Chapter 18 provide you with practical applications of the current corporate governance issues and offer trouble-shooting strategies for dealing with such issues as compliance advice.

Other features of *SCG*

The other features of *SCG* designed to optimise its usefulness to you and your business are the following:

- chapter templates: corporate governance templates are provided at the end of Chapters 4 to 15 inclusive;
- glossary: there is a glossary of key terms and expressions concerning the corporate governance field;

- questions and answers: two chapters contain 'question and answer' sections to allow you quickly to identify significant issues and to determine the corporate governance issues of premium importance for your business;
- corporate governance contemporary issues: each substantive chapter gives you guidance on the main contemporary corporate governance issues;
- corporate governance future trends: emerging and future corporate governance issues are spotlighted in the substantive chapters and especially in Chapter 17;
- bibliography: there is a bibliography at the end of *SCG*.

Getting value out of this book

SCG is designed for you to be able to refer to it at your convenience. There is a comprehensive index at the end of the book, along with a glossary of terms. By reference to the glossary, you should be in a position quickly to identify:

- the key concerns for your business;
- if there is actually a corporate governance issue or problem looming;
- and analyse corporate governance risk assessment;
- the priorities for your company;
- and implement a corporate governance management plan;
- and act on a solution-based strategy.

With the corporate governance field developing so rapidly, and with the combined output of reports and documentation running to several hundred pages, it may well be the case that your company requires specialist accounting, audit or legal advice to address your business's corporate governance concerns. As a management briefing, *SCG* can point you in the right direction and enable you to ask value-added questions of your advisers. *SCG* also aims to give you and your company some appreciation of the corporate governance trends being established; it is, as we shall see, a 'moving target' for modern management.

2

UK corporate governance: scene setting

Overview   9

What is corporate governance?   9

The origins of UK corporate governance: the 1980s   11

The 1990s: 'kinder, gentler'   14

What are the main corporate governance models?   16

The UK corporate governance 'business efficient' model   17

Questions and answers: overview of corporate governance issues   18

Why take corporate governance seriously?   19

Overview

In this chapter (and in Chapter 9) we look at the corporate governance 'big picture' and consider, amongst others, the following questions:

- where has corporate governance come from?
- what are the forces and dynamics at work behind the scenes?
- why has it taken its particular shape and direction?
- what are the contemporary corporate governance conditions?; and
- what are the emerging themes?

What is corporate governance?

A basic definition of UK corporate governance, which was provided in the Cadbury Report of 1992 (and endorsed recently by the Hampel Final Report of January 1998), is as follows:

> Corporate governance is the system by which companies are directed and controlled[1]

This definition encapsulates the basic paradox at play in corporate governance. That is, the distinction between, on the one hand, the broad notion of profit, directed and managed by the board of directors and senior management, striving to maximise shareholder returns, as against broader control and overseeing concerns which essentially seek to place the company or the business within a larger framework. The profit concern revolves around the question 'what is the company doing?', whereas the control question becomes, 'how is the company going about making its profit?'.

The divergence between these questions lies at the heart of the joint stock company from its inception as a trading vehicle in the fifteenth and sixteenth century when the first such companies (for example, the Dutch East Indies company) divided the issues of ownership of the company (the shareholders or stockholders) and the management of the company. In terms of those early companies, there was literally a divide of several thousands of miles between owners and managers.

The eighteenth-century economist Adam Smith recognised the fundamental problems and paradoxes which emanate from the fact that there is, in companies, a separation between:

- beneficial ownership; and
- executive decision-making.

Given the fundamental distinction between the two concerns of profit and control, it is no wonder that formulating an agreed definition of 'corporate governance' is not considered a high priority. There are, however, vehement arguments as to what corporate governance involves in terms of its contemporary ambit. It can be given both a narrow and a broad definition. A narrow definition of corporate governance would involve placing a few checks and balances on the board of directors by, principally, the shareholders.

On the other hand, a broad definition of corporate governance would encapsulate virtually every aspect of company behaviour by placing the company within a complex web or matrix of its various stakeholders, including shareholders, employees, customers, competitors, environmental interests, regulators, government agencies, etc.

The 1990s have represented the basic mapping out of the corporate governance project. The next decade will see the shape of that project becoming more defined, as the term 'corporate governance' assumes an established place in the contemporary business environment.

Some of the discernible aspects of corporate governance which have emerged are as follows:

Balancing management and planning

Corporate governance recognises that the company, through its board, has two key aspects to its work: day-to-day management and longer-term planning.

It recognises the need to find a balance between the company's need to make a profit and the company's duty to be accountable. In this broad sense, corporate governance can be seen as creating the sphere in which business operates; it provides the ethical framework by which companies make their profits and carry out their business plans.

Business ethics

Corporate governance can be likened to a business ethics navigation system. It can operate within the broader framework of the corporate environment and the market place – it is not an end in itself but a means to an end (as the recent Hampel Report confirms).

A means, not an end

Because corporate governance operates in response to companies (and not the other way around), and because companies themselves are artificial entities who can only trade, make contracts, pursue business plans through 'people', e.g. the directors and the shareholders, describing the corporate governance system necessarily means identifying the various roles of those people both inside and outside the company. Hence *SCG* involves briefly describing the roles of the directors, shareholders, employees, auditors (and others involved in the operation and control of companies) in terms of the overall corporate governance matrix.

Finding UK corporate governance

Q: Where is UK corporate governance to be found?

A: Primarily in the three main reports which, together, map out UK corporate governance.

They are:

(a) the Cadbury Report of 1992;

(b) the Greenbury Report of 1995; and

(c) the Hampel Report of 1998.

These three reports are specifically considered in Chapter 3.

The origins of UK corporate governance: the 1980s

It is no coincidence that corporate governance is essentially a 1990s phenomenon. This is principally for one fairly compelling reason: the heady 1980s. It can be argued that each decade encapsulates its own set of key markers: its social, cultural, economic labels. For instance, the 1960s were encapsulated by concepts such as 'hippy', 'civil rights', 'sexual liberation' and 'pop music', and the 1970s by 'flares', 'Vietnam' and 'disco' and 'rock'. And the 1980s? The decade can fit neatly around the images of 'greed' and 'excess'.

Popular cultural perceptions of the 1980s

The 1980s were, and have come to be encapsulated by, the term 'greed is good', uttered by Gordon Gecko played by Michael Douglas in the Hollywood-produced hit movie *Wall Street* (made in 1987 and directed by Oliver Stone). Even before the decade had finished, its greed was legendary and stamped indelibly over the decade like some form of cattle-brand.

The movie *Wall Street* was one of a string of films and popular cultural depictions of business: money, profit and greed as the ultimate accolades, as the fruits of the orchard and, if getting them meant paying any price: deceiving colleagues, firing employees, etc., then so be it.

Companies were portrayed as environments where ethics were not perceived. Michael Milken and junk bonds. Borrowing against non-existent assets; trading in non-existent shares; selling before you'd paid for something; cherry-picking assets, laying off swathes of long-serving employees.

Company law was perceived to be like a war zone: amoral, ruthless and rule-less; run by remorseless mercenaries only out for themselves and the 'bottom line'.

The media's preoccupation with the 1980s 'corporate cowboys'

Think of the corporate excesses of the 1980s – Guinness, Polly Peck, Maxwell and BCCI in the UK; Boesky, junk bonds' king Michael Milken in the United States; Bond, Skase and Elliott in Australia. The 'greed is good' society had its globe-strutting gods in every western country; its high-risk, high rolling, wrong side of the law corporate cowboys. Companies looked more like the wild-west town of yesteryear with a sheriff departed from town and no law, and certainly no ethics in sight. It was a decade also summed up by the Warren Zevon song 'Lawyers, Guns and Money', i.e. hire a good takeover specialist and go in and ruthlessly take over any company for which you can get sufficient borrowings.

Now, corporate news angles are quite different. In the late 1990s when there is talk of a major merger or acquisition of one company by another, the question of employees is prominent. Will a so-called 'rationalisation' involve several thousand people losing their jobs? If that is to be the case, is the takeover or merger a good thing? Whereas the 1980s were marked by economic rationalism which involved a very narrow set of inputs (chiefly concerning profit), the 1990s has seen the broadening of the parameters, so that an issue such as a takeover or a merger involves a far more complex set of questions beyond the simple one of profit and business rationality. The 1990s have seen the coming together of the 'commercial' with the 'moral' as far as business is concerned.

The UK 1980s phenomenon: privatisation

The 1980s also saw a sea-change in the way the UK government operated and saw its role in terms of the broader economic and social context. Again, one word or concept encompasses the change: 'privatisation'. Douglas Hurd, Foreign Minister in the Major government, and a long-standing cabinet member, described his own government's agenda memorably as one of 'perpetual revolution'.

The ambit of government at the start of the 1980s was vastly different by the early 1990s. Electricity, aircraft, telecommunications, gas, water, trains, prisons, nuclear power, and coal have all, to some extent, left the state sector and re-emerged in the private sector. This phenomenon has changed the face of government; it has also had both a profound and irreversible effect on the way in which business is done. The company climate has permanently altered as a result.

The privatisation phenomenon has influenced the way companies operate in several ways.

(a) Managers and owners: the manner in which companies operate. The gap between 'management' and 'ownership', traditionally large, has narrowed appreciably so that the board must work and be seen to work more closely with shareholders.

(b) Broader contexts: the broadening of the constraints in which companies operate. Companies now have to regard not just economic criteria, the narrow concept of profit and the bottom line but a complex web of social, ethical, environmental and even political contexts and considerations.

(c) Regulatory frameworks: the transfer from state ownership to public ownership of industries such as British Telecom, British Gas and British Rail has focused attention on two matters particularly:

   (i) finding the appropriate regulatory framework for such companies; and

   (ii) setting the appropriate levels of reward for the directors of newly privatised companies.

Privatisation and PR

Companies such as British Rail and British Gas have been regarded, by virtue of their histories as part of the government, as 'political', certainly for the first few years after they went public. They are in a hybrid position: whilst the managers and board view them as commercial entities with new working charters, the public's focus is on their histories and their traditional roles as providers of essential services. It is this fundamental gap in perceptions which has underpinned much of the debate (often heated, as with recent British Gas annual general meetings and Rail inquiries into safety issues, etc.) when it involves such companies.

The regulatory model for privatised companies

The regulatory model now in operation is for each privatised 'industry' to have in place a regulator who oversees the general performance of such companies and balances the interests of the company, the management, and the shareholders, on the one hand, against the interests of consumers on the other. These industries are in their infancy. Take British Gas, for example. It is only recently that the supply of gas to homes has become competitive, as BG's monopoly is challenged.

Such industries are also volatile as they go through growth stages: witness water and electricity, as issues of cross-ownership emerge and electricity companies seek to link up with water companies.

As such industries mature, the time from when they were state owned will correspondingly increase, and the perceptions of management and the public will no doubt change. They will gradually shed their hybrid status with changes in personnel, for example, as new managers with no working experience of pre-privatisation become more prevalent on the board, and the public's perception will alter, no doubt.

But it can certainly be said that, if privatisation has created a singly damaging image problem for privatised companies in particular, and public companies in general, it has been the issue of directors' pay. The issue of the salary packages on offer to the directors of newly privatised companies has continued to dog some privatised industries, notably water and gas. This was the key motivation behind the second major corporate governance report: the Greenbury Report.

The 1990s: 'kinder, gentler'

For much of the early 1990s, the UK economy was in prolonged recession characterised by many company failures, high unemployment, low inflation, and the absence of a feel-good factor for consumers.

It was a time of reflection and reconsideration for many companies; the spirit of post-1980s renewal was encapsulated by another catch-phrase originating in the USA – this time from the speech writers of President George Bush, when he invoked the image of 'a kinder, gentler' America.

Just as with privatisation, the recession, which was characterised by large numbers of employees losing their jobs, coincided with the perception that directors were awarding themselves large salary packages. Company boards were seen as out of touch, as unfeeling. They were portrayed as being insensitive to shareholders or employers, in terms of the company or in wider terms, including social effects.

Globalisation

As the UK economy emerged from recession, the new 'buzz' concept was 'globalisation', fuelled by developments such as the worldwide launch of products such as Windows 95 and the exponential growth in the Internet.

The features of globalisation

'Globalisation' has become a key concept of the 1990s. It defies simple definition but includes the following traits:

(a) the increasingly interconnected nature of state economic systems;

(b) the increasing influence of multinational companies;

(c) the (arguably) diminishing influence of 'states' as economic, legal and political entities at the expense of companies; and

(d) the increasing influence of networked communication and commerce systems, e.g. the Net, e-mail.

Globalisation as it affects companies

As the western world's economy has become increasingly global in outlook, this has had profound effects on the way that companies operate. For instance:

(a) for employees, job security has become a key concern.

(b) for managers and employers, strategic growth and the search for new markets and competitive cost structures have become the key concerns.

(c) for shareholders, premium returns are sought in markets as likely to be 'far afield' as at home, as fund managers and others adopt global investment hedging strategies.

European integration

There has, of course, been another issue of importance affecting UK management, and that is Europe and the increasing 'convergence' of the domestic laws of the member states (including Britain) under the Treaty of Rome. This has meant that business with an

EU dimension (i.e. involving trade with a group or body in another EU state) has become increasingly subject to EU regulations and directives.

Commercial dimensions to doing business in Europe

In terms of a UK-based company appointing a distributor of its products in France, the situation regulating exactly what the appointing company can require of the distributor will be governed by Article 85 of the Treaty of Rome. This means, for example, that the UK company cannot give compulsory directions on prices to be charged but is merely able to make recommendations. In addition to price positions, a whole raft of other commercial matters needs to be considered.

Another example of the EU influence is where a company in the UK appoints a 'commercial agent' (required to be self-employed). Regard will be had to the commercial agents' directive which is based on the German domestic model and has since become the EU's blueprint for application in member states. The 'harmonisation' of laws will continue as an integral process of economic and monetary union. The process will inevitably be speeded up by monetary union.

The EU and UK company law

In terms of company law developments, it has been the continental model which has led to one-shareholder companies being allowed under the Companies Act 1985.

The EU and UK corporate governance

In terms of the UK corporate governance debate, the continental 'board of directors' model (known as two-tier where management and direction are officially split) has been rejected by, for instance, the Hampel Report, which endorses the UK traditional model known as the 'unitary' structure (where management and direction are unified). For further discussion of this, see Chapter 4.

What are the main corporate governance models?

Q1: Returning to the UK domestic governance scene, what in broad terms are the available models of governance?

A1: In broad terms, we could identify three on a spectrum.

At one extreme – the 'no governance' model

'No governance' would involve the concept of boardroom freedom, subject only to legal and statutory regulation. The emergence of corporate governance over a 6- or 7-year-period in the UK means that this scenario is no longer a realistic option; corporate governance is now a UK corporate reality.

At the other extreme – a rule-bound, box-ticking model

This model would promote corporate governance into an end-game rather than a means to an end. Such a model would be so preoccupied with ethical imperatives that it would seriously undermine the basis on which companies operate and seek prosperity for their shareholders and employees. It would militate against decisive board action; the propeller driving the business forward would become clogged. This 'pervasive governance' approach would view all recommendations as rules and regulations; the company would be inundated with paperwork leading to inefficiency and a lack of manoeuvrability.

These two models are at either end of the spectrum of possible models. A third model exists.

The middle ground: the business efficient model

This model recognises that a broad notion of 'corporate ethics' is actually seen as important, whilst at the same time balancing against that ethical objective the aspirations of companies to make a profit and to keep shareholders, employees, customers and others content. This 'balanced model' is the emerging UK corporate governance model, which is presently being mapped out.

The UK corporate governance 'business efficient' model

All three corporate governance reports and most particularly the latest, the Hampel Report, have signalled their intention for corporate governance to avoid clogging the wheels of commerce with burdensome regulations, with management looking over the shoulder, and the encouragement of box-ticking in their approach to corporate governance issues.

This approach is underpinned by the firm belief that corporate governance is:

- a navigation system;
- an aid to doing business better;

- a set of practices for businesses to be aware of, and to factor into their strategies;

but not:

- a substitute for doing business, i.e. not a end in itself;
- intended to be overly burdensome so that management is constantly looking over its shoulder to comply with corporate governance performing the role of a comprehensive and compulsory code of conduct.

Balance

Inherent in the UK model is a continual balancing act between 'over-governance' and 'under-governance'.

The practical compliance model requires:

(a) a broad understanding of where corporate governance is 'coming from' and 'going to';

(b) an appreciation of the 'hit-list' of corporate governance issues, i.e. the hot topics and emerging topics; and

(c) a PR strategy which effectively communicates the company's corporate governance approach, which optimises the business's brand image as 'corporate governance responsible' rather than 'corporate governance reckless'.

The UK corporate governance model is discussed further in Chapter 3.

Questions and answers: overview of corporate governance issues

Q1: How does corporate governance differ from management?

A1: Corporate governance encompasses both management and broader concepts of strategy and business direction.

Q2: What are the main sources of corporate governance?

A2: The three reports and their trickle-down effect into areas like the Stock Exchange Listing Rules.

Q3: What are the current trends?

A3: In the latest report, the Hampel Committee suggests that corporate governance may have shifted too much towards regulation, what it calls 'accountability' at the expense of 'business prosperity'. Accountability it says 'has preoccupied much public debate over the past few years. We would wish to see the balance corrected.'[2]

Q4: Are there parallels to company corporate governance in other fields?

A4: Yes; take newspapers and their code of self-regulation, implemented and amended from time to time by the Press Complaints Commission (for example, privacy issues have been tightened in the light of Diana, Princess of Wales). This is an initiative of the industry, just as the corporate governance project has been.

Q5: Is any of corporate governance compulsory?

A5: Yes; this is more likely for listed companies in that, for example, the Stock Exchange has formalised recommendations by adopting them as conditions of listing.

Why take corporate governance seriously?

The answer to this question is a book in itself. Some of the facets of the answer explored throughout this book are as follows.

(a) Businesses today operate in what we might call intensive stakeholding environments.

(b) Litigation concerning business is a growing trend.

(c) Ethics and ethical concerns are now, more than ever, associated with company action and direction; think of Shell and the Brent Spar oil rig fiasco. Whatever the actual environmental and scientific merits of deep-sea sinking of the rig, Shell's actions were portrayed as the irresponsible dumping of industrial waste, and the whole agenda was taken from its hands. The story became one of corporate greed and profligacy against which Shell was rendered powerless.

(d) Media images are vitally important to a company; the media possesses the ability to change perceptions overnight; just ask the directors of Newcastle United PLC.

We examine some of these issues in the case studies of Chapter 18.

Notes

1 Cadbury Report, paragraph 2.5.

2 Hampel Report, page 7.

3

The corporate governance jigsaw: pieces, players and issues

Overview 23

The key UK corporate governance issues 24

The corporate governance pieces 24

The Cadbury Report 1992 24

The Greenbury Report 1995 26

The Hampel Report 1998 27

The key players 28

Questions and answers: pieces, players and issues 29

Themes of the UK corporate governance emerging model 32

Overview

This chapter deals with the big picture of the UK corporate governance jigsaw. It focuses on three key aspects:

(a) the main documentation involved in corporate governance;

(b) the key participants in corporate governance; and

(c) the main issues arising in the corporate governance model, which has been developed as a result of the main documentation.

Documentation

This chapter gives an overview of the three main documents making up corporate governance. These are the reports of the Cadbury, the Greenbury and the Hampel Committees, named after their respective chairmen.

Key participants

The chapter identifies the main players in terms of corporate governance implementation. If we think of corporate governance as a stakeholding system, we can draw a distinction between three separate groups of stakeholders:

(a) the company's corporate governance providers, notably the board and company secretary;

(b) the company's corporate governance consumers, notably the shareholders and employees; and

(c) the regulators of the company's corporate governance, notably Companies House and the Stock Exchange.

Groups (a) and (b) are internal constituents of the company. Group (c) is external to it. Chapters in this book deal separately with each of these stakeholders and with their role in the corporate governance matrix.

Key themes

We briefly look at some of the themes underpinning the development of the UK's governance model before examining specific issues concerning the key participants involved in the operations of companies.

The key UK corporate governance issues

The key corporate governance issues reflect the concerns motivating the reports and why they came into being.

They include:

(a) communication: effective boardroom communication with shareholders, employees, and others;

(b) sensitivity: boardroom 'sensitivity', for instance, in relation to salary packages for directors;

(c) accountability: having better internal and external audit and other financial controls;

(d) efficiency: having better-run boards by, for instance, having a well-informed, expert, robust-minded and independent non-executive element on the board;

(e) awareness of publicity: companies in general (and boards, in particular) need to pay close attention to the publicity angles of what they are seeking to achieve.

In all these issues, corporate governance emerges as:

- an adjunct to business; not a substitute for it;
- a route-map, planner and guide to enhancing the prospects of business prosperity.

The corporate governance pieces

The primary pieces of UK corporate governance are the three reports known as:

- The Cadbury Report 1992;
- The Greenbury Report 1995;
- The Hampel Report 1998.

We will look at each of these in turn, and then apply various issues in relation to specific corporate governance stakeholders in later chapters of the book.

The Cadbury Report 1992

(a) The Cadbury Committee, chaired by Sir Adrian Cadbury;

(b) Set up in May 1991; reported in December 1992;

(c) Set up by the Financial Reporting Council, the London Stock Exchange and the accountancy profession;

(d) Formal name of final documentation:

   (i) *The Code of Best Practice re The Financial Aspects of Corporate Governance* (12 pages)

   (ii) *The Financial Aspects of Corporate Governance – Full Report* (91 pages).

Main reason for being set up

The key issue of concern, into which Cadbury looked, was the spate of large-scale corporate failures stemming from business practices which were prevalent in the 1980s and exacerbated by the recession of the early 1990s. Three specific instances of corporate excess are specifically mentioned in the preface to the Cadbury Report. These are:

(a) the Bank of Credit and Commerce International (BCCI) which went into liquidation in 1991, involving the loss of millions of pounds of depositors' funds;

(b) the group of companies dominated by Robert Maxwell and the 'disappearance' of pension funds; and

(c) the controversy over the size of directors' remuneration packages (largely fuelled by newly privatised companies seeking to establish 'going market rate' principles for their particular industries).

Key outcomes

(a) Code of Best Practice and compliance statements. All listed companies after June 1993 need to include a Code of Best Practice and a compliance statement in their annual financial reports and give reasons for any areas of non-compliance.

(b) Auditors to have the chance to review the compliance statement before publication so that it can be objectively verified (this stresses the underlying need for the auditors to be independent of the company – see Chapter 10).

(c) London Stock Exchange Listing Rules to require compliance statements. In order for a company to be listed it must publish the statement of compliance (reviewed by the auditors).

Next steps

Cadbury recommended a new committee to be set up by June 1995 (i.e. this was to become the Greenbury Committee).

The Greenbury Report 1995

(a) The Greenbury Committee, chaired by Sir Richard Greenbury, Chairman of Marks and Spencer;

(b) Set up in January 1995; reported in July 1995;

(c) Set up on the recommendation of the Cadbury Report and through an initiative of the CBI;

(d) Formal name of final documentation *Directors' Remuneration – Report of a Study Group chaired by Sir Richard Greenbury* (59 pages).

Main reason for being set up

The Greenbury focus was the board and its perceived PR failings in relation to pay packages and communication. The following issues are highlighted in Sir Richard Greenbury's preface to the final report:

(a) directors' pay – full disclosure;

(b) better board accountability structures;

(c) improved alignment of director and shareholder interests;

(d) more effective implementation of board responsibility.

Key outcomes

Greater boardroom pay transparency. For example, on executive pay, detailed disclosure was required by listed companies. This involved breaking the package down into its component parts, including:

- basic salary;
- benefits in kind;
- annual bonus;
- share options;
- other long-term incentives;
- pension rights;
- a report by the remuneration committee.

These matters, in turn, became a requirement of the listing rules for those companies going public.[1]

Next steps

The Greenbury next steps included:

(a) having the Stock Exchange and other bodies implement certain of the proposals, such as the disclosures on boardroom pay and other requirements (as per above); and

(b) follow up with the Hampel Report.

The Greenbury Report is discussed further in Chapter 4, dealing with corporate governance issues and the board.

The Hampel Report 1998

(a) The Hampel Committee, chaired by Sir Ronnie Hampel, Chairman of ICI;

(b) Set up in November 1995; reported in July 1997 (interim basis) and January 1998 (final report);

(c) Set up on the recommendation of the Greenbury Report by the Financial Reporting Council;

(d) Formal name of final documentation: *Committee on Corporate Governance: Final Report*, January 1998 (66 pages).

Main reason for being set up

To continue the monitoring and refining of the UK corporate governance model.

Key outcomes

Among the Hampel Report's key recommendations are the following:

(a) business prosperity as well as accountability: to steer the public debate back towards business prosperity as well as accountability;

(b) unitary boards: to keep unitary boards continental-style; two-tier boards rejected;

(c) non-executive directors to make up at least one-third of board, i.e. independence stressed, with auditors independence as a theme;

(d) the roles of company chairman and chief executive to be separate;

(e) no shareholder vote on director remuneration;

(f) companies should give business presentations at AGMs and use shareholder meetings more constructively;

(g) proxy votes should be counted and declared ahead of AGM votes.

Next steps

The Hampel Report recommendations for the future shape of the corporate governance project include:

(a) a period of reflection and consolidation after the flurry of activity, i.e. three major inquiries and reports in the space of 6 years;

(b) correcting the balance away from accountability (i.e. 'over-governance') and back in favour of 'business prosperity'; and, generally,

(c) to make refinements to the present system rather than wholesale changes.

The Hampel committee will produce a set of principles taken from the three reports and pass it on to the London Stock Exchange, followed by a period of consultation allowing ambiguities to be cleared up and further specific guidance to be sought if necessary.

Following the consultation process, some matters may become incorporated in the Stock Exchange's Rules. The Hampel Report signals a continuation of public companies leading the way in terms of corporate governance, together with good practice principles being applied by other companies in response to their particular circumstances.

The key players

Having identified the triad of reports making up the centrepiece of UK corporate governance, the next step is to identify the key players in the corporate governance matrix.

This breaks down into:

(a) corporate governance providers, i.e. those responsible for corporate governance policy and compliance – principally the company board;

(b) corporate governance targets, i.e. those for whom the corporate governance project has been established – principally the shareholders;

(c) corporate governance regulators, i.e. those responsible for maintaining the corporate governance framework and compliance practices, for example, the Stock Exchange and market competitors.

Questions and answers: pieces, players and issues

We will deal with these groups in later chapters, so for now we will provide an overview of their roles, and the key pieces and issues of the corporate governance jigsaw by way of questions and answers.

Q1: Who are the key players in terms of corporate governance?

A1: There are several key players including:

(a) the board of directors, who are responsible for the corporate governance of the company;

(b) the company secretary, who should be fully abreast of corporate governance developments and liaise closely with the board;

(c) the shareholders, who are linked to the directors via the financial reporting system;

(d) the auditors, who provide the shareholders with an external objective check on the directors' financial statements;

(e) other concerned users, particularly employees (to whom the directors owe some responsibility), who are indirectly addressed by the financial statements.

Q2: What of those parties who are external to the company?

A2: They play an important role in various guises: as regulators; as customers, as competitors.

Q3: What are the main documents making up corporate governance?

A3: As mentioned above, there are three main reports:

(a) Cadbury Report (including *The Code of Best Practice*) 1992

(b) Greenbury Report 1995

(c) Hampel Report 1997

Q4: How do these corporate governance reports and documents fit together, i.e. what is the big picture?

A4: Essentially, the three reports act together; they overlap; therefore, they have to be read together.

Q5: Why was corporate governance put on the map in the early 1990s and why was Cadbury set up?

Solving Your Corporate Governance Issues | The corporate governance jigsaw

A5: There was a perceived lack of confidence in the financial reporting standards of companies and in the ability of auditors to provide the assurances required by the users of financial statements (see Chapter 10 on auditors).

Q6: What other problems triggered Cadbury?

A6: Issues such as the sudden collapse of companies and the responsibility of company boards. There was a general perception that standards in boardrooms in the 1990s required more readily identifiable yardsticks by which to measure collective board performance.

As mentioned earlier, the 1980s were perceived as a decade of corporate excess. Along with a proliferation of takeovers, there were swingeing job losses following mergers and takeovers.

Corporate governance, in turn, was seen as an attempt to improve shareholder, employee and customer confidence and to assist in satisfying the wider community interests such as those of companies' regulators, the Stock Exchange and the Government.

Q7: What were the Cadbury terms of reference?

A7: General: recommendations on good practice in relation to financial reporting and accountability. Specific areas to investigate include:

(a) directors: executive and non-executive directors;

(b) shareholders: reporting to shareholders and other 'financially interested parties';

(c) information to shareholders: how often, how clear, and what is the appropriate format?

(d) audit committees: should boards have them and, if yes, whom should they comprise and what should they do?

(e) auditors: their role and responsibilities;

(f) links: between the board, the shareholders and the auditors;

(g) other relevant matters.

Q8: Who is the *Code of Best Practice* aimed at?

A8: The directors of all UK companies are encouraged to use the *Code of Best Practice* for guidance.

Q9: What are the key provisions and aims of the *Code of Best Practice*?

A9: (a) Statements of Compliance. In accounts since the end of 1992 to include:

- a statement of compliance, i.e. that the company has complied with the code;
- to provide reasons for any non-compliance.

(b) Preliminary review by the auditors. The statements of compliance should only be published after review by the auditors. The details of the auditors' review is decided on by the auditing practices board.

(c) Compliance pressure. Pressure should be brought on the board by all relevant parties to ensure compliance with the code. This particularly includes those with considerable power, i.e. institutional investors (fund managers, pensions managers, etc.).

Q10: Is the *Code of Best Practice* compulsory?

A10: Yes, for PLCs where listing and other authorities have enacted its provisions and made them a condition of listing; but generally not otherwise.

Q11: Is corporate governance compulsory?

A11: Generally no, unless we have a situation such as in *A10* above. The Hampel Report is at pains to point out the sensible, company-by-company approach to corporate governance issues which should be adopted. Corporate governance is designed to work alongside and assist business, not to hamper it.

Q12: What is happening in terms of the corporate governance 'big picture' presently?

A12: Corporate governance is going through a period of consolidation and fine-tuning. There are no major initiatives because the key building blocks are considered to be in place. It's a question now of amending at the margins; of making corporate governance practical and of satisfying the various demands of those within companies and the interests of 'community' stakeholders such as regulators.

The Hampel Report has signalled that it will be the last for some time; it heralds a slow-down in the corporate governance project.

Q13: Current and future trends – what sort of issues will affect the shape of corporate governance?

A13: In no particular order, the following sorts of dynamics occurring in the market place–business community:

- high profile corporate collapses;
- privatisations and issues such as 'is the public getting value for money?' and safety issues;
- 'Fat cats' – pay; profits; takeover bonanza;
- public perceptions generally and PR angles;

- recession, economic slow-downs and unemployment;
- global shocks, e.g. the Asian crisis and re-evaluation of corporate approaches and values;
- 'shareholder democracy' and new technology, e.g. better informed and more articulate shareholders;
- institutional shareholders–asset managers becoming quasi-market-regulators; acting as bottom-line realists rather than as loyalty stockholders in relation to the company.

Themes of the UK corporate governance emerging model

Some of the themes of contemporary UK governance include the following:

Is corporate governance a 'natural' outcome of a mature economy?

It could be argued that corporate governance, as it has developed in the UK, can be seen as a naturally occurring part of a mature capitalist economy (such as the UK's). See Chapter 17 for further discussion of this argument.

Business-driven (i.e. corporate governance as a 'bottom-up' model)

One of the increasingly important traits of 1990s corporate life is the question of 'who exactly is driving a given agenda?'. Corporate governance, as a project, can be seen as a business-driven initiative. The three reports have been set up by business in response to perceived 'business problems'. This has been vitally important in terms of the corporate governance shape, to date, and its future direction. What we have witnessed in the UK is a bottom-up model where business has essentially been seen to be pro-active and responsible rather than reactive or disinterested. The agenda has not been top-down, i.e. imposed by government or other public bodies.

Market-driven rather than rule-bound

Whether business will retain essential control of the emerging model of corporate governance will depend on many matters and principally on the question of whether the present government overhauls company legislation in any major way. If it does so it may be tempted to promote corporate governance in legislative form so that it becomes a series of compulsory rules and regulations rather than a bottom-up, business-driven initiative.

Confusing 'detailed codes' with 'general principles'

The Hampel Report alludes to the fact that there appears to be confusion over corporate governance, with many businesses promoting 'recommendations' and guidance on firm rules where they are left without discretion as to whether to implement them or not.

The Hampel Report specifically endorses a flexible, common-sense approach to application of the principles, which bears in mind a company's particular circumstances.[2]

The Hampel Report distinguishes between detailed codes, on the one hand, and general principles on the other, by drawing a distinction between the questions the board should be asking of itself:

(a) with detailed codes such as Cadbury and Greenbury, the board should ask itself the question: 'how far are they complied with?'

(b) with principles, the right question is: 'how are they applied in practice?' i.e. principles allow a company-wide discretion to apply them sensibly in light of their circumstances.[3]

Balance as a theme

As we have noted, the Cadbury, Greenbury and Hampel Reports share one overriding theme, and that is of 'balance', i.e. each report individually, and the reports collectively, seek to find a balance between:

(a) the model of the 'free market'; and

(b) the model of the highly 'regulated' market.

The three reports have sought to map out what might be described as an 'ethically informed, capitalist-efficient' hybrid model of corporate governance that sits somewhere in the centre ground of the spectrum between the two extremes.

The Cadbury Report, for example, talks of 'striking the right balance' between control over business and 'retaining the essential spirit of enterprise', on the one hand, against 'public accountability' and 'meeting the standards of corporate governance now expected of them' on the other hand.[4]

The Hampel Report talks of balancing business accountability and prosperity[5] and in fact of 'correcting the balance' back in favour of business prosperity.

Ongoing corporate governance themes

The three corporate governance reports recognise that:

(a) there is an ongoing tension, dialogue and debate between the two models;

(b) the ideal business environment lies somewhere on the spectrum between the two extremes;

(c) a market in an advanced capital system cannot be completely 'free', i.e. it isn't a Darwinian jungle where the strong survive and the weak perish;

(d) corporate ethics is not about box-ticking, or 'looking over the shoulder' because this means that a business is not doing what it exists to do, i.e. make returns for shareholders subject to the agreed parameters;

(e) the corporate governance good practice model is not fixed in stone; it is emerging; over time the corporate governance model is tinkered with, grafted on, shaped, sculpted to meet the needs of changing times.

The emerging UK model is becoming increasingly influential on the international stage, as other countries come on-stream with their own corporate governance projects.

Notes

1 Listing Rule 12.43(x) as per Hampel Report, page 37.

2 Hampel Report, page 10.

3 Hampel Report, page 16.

4 Cadbury Report, page 11.

5 Hampel Report, page 7.

4

Corporate governance for the board: general issues

Overview   37

The director's role in the company   37

The board's role   37

Distinguishing management from governance   38

The management–governance spectrum   38

The board's 'specific' role and 'context' role   39

The board and the stakeholders   41

The directors' legal position   43

The board's role in corporate governance   44

Applicability of corporate governance for listed and non-listed companies   45

Corporate governance issues summary for the board   46

Corporate governance issues for the board *vis-à-vis* a specific director   49

Non-executive directors   52

Compliance strategies for the board   54

Boardroom template for corporate governance   56

Overview

In this chapter we examine the role played by a company's board in terms of the corporate governance issues confronting them and the implementation of practical and time–resource efficient solutions to such problems. We look at the following aspects of the board–corporate governance relationship:

- the role of the board as a collective entity;
- the role of an individual director; and
- the role of the company secretary.

The director's role in the company

Each director individually (and the board collectively) plays a pivotal role in terms of the operation of the company for whom, and by whom, they are employed. This double-barrelled relationship, i.e. 'for whom and by whom' means that directors are referred to in law as 'fiduciaries' to the company. As we shall examine briefly below, on page 43, they must maintain high standards of performance, competence and honesty at all times.

The board's role

Collectively, the board is responsible for:

- day-to-day management, for example, keeping the various sub-divisions of the company – manufacturing, finance, marketing, sales, and so on working – smoothly and attending to employee concerns;
- longer-term strategy and planning, for example, looking beyond the current financial year; refining and adapting market strategies;
- trouble-shooting: this may involve many aspects. It may be in terms of pre-empting and either avoiding or solving potential problems, for example, anticipating busy sales periods and having sufficient stock or, conversely, retracting stock levels during quiet periods; dealing with environmentally contaminated land and other assets; early and clear communication with shareholders, employees and other stakeholders;
- 'fire-fighting': this may simply be advanced 'trouble-shooting'. Again, it may involve many and various aspects in terms of dealing with actual or imminent problems, for example experiencing cash flow problems, etc. requiring careful strategic planning

and possible emergency measures to be put in place: asset sales, creditors meetings, and so on.

Distinguishing management from governance

The above list of directorial concerns is obviously not exhaustive.

Nor are these board roles necessarily 'discrete'; they may well overlap. The company is, after all, a 'moving' entity; problems (just like employees) come and go; the picture is never a static one.

Another way of seeing the tasks above, and the function of the board in general, is to distinguish between two broad types of directorial responsibility:

(a) management; and

(b) governance.

The board's management role

This connotes the day-to-day aspects of the business, the performance of sub-divisions of the company; essentially it looks at each of the various pieces of the jigsaw making up the company.

The board's governance role

This refers to a role over and above the management role; if management is largely concerned with 'detail', i.e. the minutiae of the business and its component parts, governance is concerned with the 'big picture', i.e. the broader concept of the company's rationale for doing business and its strategic position in the market place.

The management–governance spectrum

What we have in the space between the management and governance roles is a recognition that companies operate within both 'narrow' and 'broad' parameters. Essentially, what we find is that, for each and every company, the 'management' concept occupies one end of the spectrum and the 'governance' concept the other end of the spectrum (see Fig. 4.1).

Figure 4.1
The management–governance spectrum

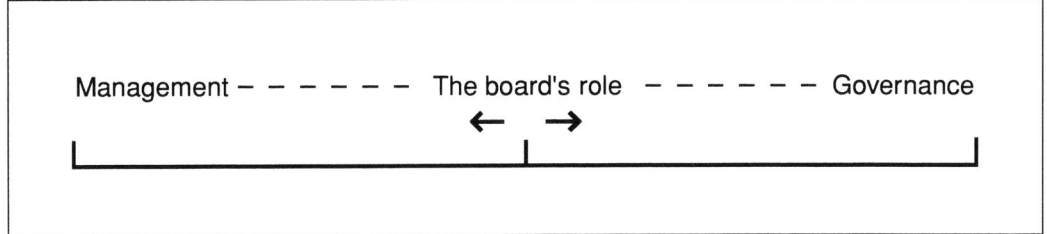

The key and continuing task for the board of every company (from a 'day 1' private company to a multinational) is to monitor the management–governance mix so as to act in the best interests of the shareholders.

Each company board needs to adjust its mix of management and governance, i.e. to be continually monitoring its place on the management–governance spectrum.

The two tasks of management and governance go together and, in fact, one cannot exist without the other. That is, a company cannot be '100 per cent management concerned', for it would be completely failing to appreciate the 'business environment' in which it operates and to which it must pay attention. Nor can a company be '100 per cent governance oriented'. If it were, it would be so concerned about the business environment and the context in which it operated that it would disregard the very reasons for being in business: survival, the bottom line, breaking even and shareholder profit.

The board's role is to get the balance correct between management and governance, whether it's 60 management/40 governance, 70/30, 80/20 and so on. The management–governance mix is not going to be static; it will shift from year to year or respond in light of 'major' company events. Those 'events' themselves will range from 'shocks' such as financial and cash-flow problems within the company to 'good news' events – major contracts being entered into, premium sales and other 'bonus' occurrences.

The board's 'specific' role and 'context' role

An alternative way of viewing the 'spectrum' facing each board is to define the management role as the board's 'specific' role and the governance criteria as its 'general' role (see Fig. 4.2).

Just as with management and governance, the board must simultaneously fulfil both the 'specific role' and the 'context role', as well as continually refining the ongoing mix between the two roles.

Figure 4.2
The board's 'specific' role and 'context' role

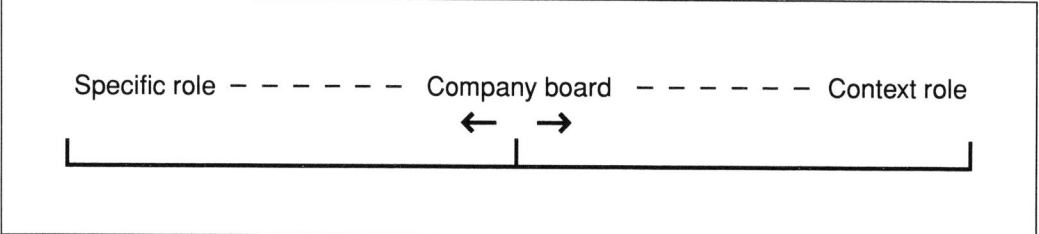

The board's specific role

The narrow parameters, what we might call each company's 'specificity role', include:

- the promotion of the core business product or specific services provided; and
- ensuring the loyalty and satisfaction of the specific customer base, and so on.

The board's context function

The broader parameters, what we might call the 'context role', refer to the fact that the board has to continually be aware of, monitor and respond to other contexts – other issues. The specificity function of each company does not operate in a vacuum, but in the light of broader, 'other context' issues, for example, the company's competitors, its environmental, political, social and other concerns. A recent and graphic illustration of these broader context functions confronting a board is provided by McDonald's UK. The McDonald's Board has recently had to work to counter two 'shock' context events – the BSE cattle crisis with its associated consumer crisis of confidence in beef products, and the longest-running case in legal history, the so-called McLibel case recently concluded broadly in McDonald's favour.[1]

Another example is Shell's episode with the Brent Spar oil rig and its tussle with Greenpeace. Shell, as a multinational, has a complex matrix of national as well as environmental concerns, to which it must be seen to be sensitive.

Environmental sensitivity appears to be pervasive as a general concern; note the fact that the Body Shop Group has recently been picketed by environmental lobby groups; this must be partly because the Body Shop Group holds itself out as ethically unimpeachable and hence becomes something of a 'tall poppy' to knock down.

The board and the stakeholders

The board occupies the key site at the confluence of stakeholder concerns. The stakeholder concept can be seen as referring to three different groups:

- those internal to the company;
- the business-driven stakeholders; and
- the regulatory stakeholders.

This 'broad view' of stakeholders is specifically adopted in the Hampel Report where the committee writes:

> A company must develop relationships relevant to its success. This will depend on the nature of the company's business; but they will include those with employees, customers, suppliers, credit providers, local communities and governments (page 12, Hampel Report)

Internal company stakeholders

In legal terms the board owes its main responsibilities of competence and honesty to the 'company', i.e. shareholders and employees.

Shareholders

The 'company' translates in a primary sense into the shareholders (broadly both present and future shareholders). This is the case as set out by the common law (judge-made law) and confirmed in s.309 of the Companies Act 1985. (The shareholders' role in the corporate governance matrix is dealt with in Chapter 14.)

Employees

The 'company' translates in a secondary sense into the interests of the employees. This is confirmed in s.309 of the Companies Act 1985 which states:

> the matters to which the directors of a company are to have regard in the performance of the functions include the interests of the company's employees in general, as well as the interests of its members.

Section 309 and the common law mean that, in terms of running the business in both its management and governance aspects, i.e. day-to-day matters, in takeover negotiations, in sales of key parts of the business, in acquisitions, and so on, the board has to bear in mind the interests of the shareholders and the employees and be aware of the ramifications that their actions and decisions will have on these key stakeholder groups. (The employees' role in the corporate governance matrix is dealt with in Chapter 15.)

Business-driven stakeholders

Other 'stakeholders' in a broader sense are those who deal, in one capacity or another, with the company and include its business-driven stakeholders:

Creditors, i.e. banks and other lenders

Obviously, the board will need to ensure that the company can meet its debt commitments and avoid receivership or insolvency (winding up). If the directors fail in their basic duties of competence and honesty, they may become personally liable to creditors under the Insolvency Act 1986. This is especially the case under s.214 of the Insolvency Act, known as 'wrongful trading' – a situation where the company is accruing debt, but nevertheless continues to trade.

Customers, traders, suppliers, buyers, etc.

Obviously, such groups have an interest in the company's performance and continued success, especially those who are in the position of creditor.

Competitors

A company's competitors will be important; for example, their benchmarks, standards and various performance indicators set criteria against which the board can operate and the company's business plan can be executed.

The regulatory stakeholders

The third group of stakeholders is the regulatory and wider community group. It includes:

(a) Companies House and the companies regulator, who is in charge of public record keeping;

(b) the tax authorities (income tax and VAT); and

(c) receivers, liquidators and others involved in the case of a company experiencing serious financial trouble.

These groups are further discussed in Chapter 16 dealing with the company's regulators.

The directors' legal position

The legal position of company directors is set out comprehensively in Andrew Sparrow's *The Responsibilities of Company Directors* in this series of Financial Times Management Briefings.

In summary form, a director has two basic duties – competence and honesty – owed to the 'company', i.e. the shareholders and employees:

Competence

A director has a duty to be competent, i.e. to know something of the business which he or she is charged with directing. This also breaks down into the three items set out by Lord Justice Romer in *Re City Equitable Fire, 1925*,[2] a key company law case:

(a) the director does not necessarily need to be an expert in the company's business;

(b) the director does not need to attend every board meeting, but those he or she can reasonably get to; and

(c) a director is entitled to delegate tasks unless there are 'suspicious circumstances'.

Each of the three matters set out in the *Re City Equitable Fire* case will be subject to the specific requirements and documentation of a particular company. In particular, it is important to bear in mind specific matters addressed as to competence, and so on, in:

- the memorandum of association;
- the articles of association;
- any shareholder's agreement (which will supplement the articles); and
- the terms of any service agreement entered into between the director and the company.

If a director is employed or engaged on the basis of a particular competence, those matters in the *Re City Equitable Fire* case will need to be carefully reviewed.

It is also worth noting that, in light of corporate governance developments, and generally, standards expected of directors are rising not falling, so the *Re City Equitable Fire* case *de minimis* approach should not be heavily relied upon, and specific legal advice should be obtained if there is any doubt.

Honesty

The issue of a director's honesty is a matter that has been developed by case law over many years. As a fiduciary to the company, a director owes a duty of 'utmost good faith' (or *uberrimae fidae*).

Take the following example.

If AB is a director of XYZ Limited and Johnson Limited and the two companies enter a contract, AB must declare an interest at both board meetings. This is the disclosure requirement of s.317 of the Companies Act 1985 and cannot be avoided. Depending on the terms of the company's articles, AB may, or may not, be able to vote on the contract in which he is interested. (Disclosure and voting are separate issues.) Were AB not to disclose an interest in the contract, then any profit he made from the transaction would effectively be constructed as 'secret' and he would obliged to return it to the company (the law makes AB a constructive trustee; that is he holds the profit as a trustee for the beneficiary company). For further details, see Chapter 4.7 of Andrew Sparrow's *The Responsibilities of Company Directors*.[3]

The board's role in corporate governance

Vigorous debate followed by solidarity

Much like the Cabinet in the Westminster system of government with its notion of 'cabinet solidarity', the board of a company is charged by the shareholders with acting collectively, i.e. with one voice. That is not to say that there should not be vigorous debate on issues of management, policy and direction before the board reaches its majority verdict. The directors are then charged, as part of their general duty to the company, to speak with one voice (and to avoid the sort of 'memoirs after the event' approach favoured by many former cabinet members).

The three corporate governance reports (Cadbury, Greenbury and Hampel) each stress the need for independent and strong voices on the board, not simply a group which glibly agrees with the CEO or chairman.

There are, in essence, three key corporate governance strategies to meet the 'one voice – rigorous debate' board model being promoted by the reports and firmly commended by Sir Ronnie Hampel's Report published in January 1998. Those strategies concern:

(a) the separation of the tasks of CEO and chairman. These are regarded as two jobs but may, if carefully thought through and justified by the board, vest in one person;

(b) the important role of non-executive (i.e. occasional) directors on the board;

(c) the remuneration packages awarded to directors and, in particular, the issue of bonus shares to non-executive directors. The Greenbury and Cadbury Reports make recommendations as to a remuneration sub-committee on the board and the make-up of the salary package (particularly bonus shares); and

(d) sensitivity in terms of the PR ramifications of board and other decision-making. This is something we discussed in Chapter 2 and is again picked up in later chapters. It is something of a pervasive consideration for boards, especially those of listed companies.

Board diversity and differing skills

The three corporate governance reports also recognise the need for:

- diversity on the board where the needs of the business are better met; and
- different skills and perceptions to be brought to the board.

The Hampel Report makes it clear, however, that business efficacy is the yardstick for appointment when it says:

> We do not favour diversity for its own sake, to give a politically correct appearance to the list of board members or represent stakeholders (page 28, Hampel Report).

Applicability of corporate governance for listed and non-listed companies

The corporate governance reports have generally aimed themselves at listed companies. Key corporate governance requirements for listed companies have taken on the practical ramifications of having become codified and compulsory because they have been incorporated as part of the Stock Exchange Listing Rules, for example, requiring disclosure provisions as to the components of boardroom pay packages (mentioned under the Greenbury Report in Chapter 3).

It is misleading and potentially dangerous for non-listed companies simply to ignore corporate governance as an issue.

As we set out in Chapter 2, from the Cadbury Report and its *Code of Good Practice* dating from 1992, corporate governance has been seen as worthy of being adopted by all companies over time, with listed companies leading the way.

Corporate governance issues summary for the board

A summary of corporate governance related issues for any company board includes the following matters:

General approach to corporate governance: common sense and flexibility

Hampel makes it clear that it is not endorsing a 'box-ticking' approach.

The Hampel Report states as follows:

> Good corporate governance is not just a matter of prescribing particular corporate structures and complying with hard and fast rules. There is a need for broad principles. All concerned should then apply these flexibly and with common sense to the varying circumstances of individual companies.[4]

The Hampel Report is at pains to stress that it is not attempting to be some kind of all-embracing code but to provide a 'menu' of good practice for companies so as to gauge their own practices and concerns.

Corporate governance is a means and not an end.

General role of the board *vis-à-vis* the company

The board has the dual role of leadership and control, i.e. both to lead the company effectively in terms of strategy over time and to control the company on a day-to-day basis.

Corporate governance role of the board

The board's role is crucial. It is required to effectively implement corporate governance policy and strategy. The board has 'the responsibility for good corporate governance'.[5]

Written corporate governance report as part of annual report

The Hampel Report makes it a general recommendation that:

> companies should include in their annual report and accounts a narrative statement of how they apply the relevant principles (of corporate governance) to their particular circumstances.[6]

Leadership of the board

Leadership of the board resides in the chairman and CEO.

There needs to be 'high-quality' leadership in general terms.

The shape of the board: the 'unitary type' of board

The traditional UK unitary board is endorsed; not the so-called continental model which is two-tier and separates executive directors form non-executive directors so that essentially the non-executives oversee, regulate and 'second-guess' the work of executives. The Hampel Report specifically refers to the need not to over-emphasise the 'monitoring role' of the non-executive directors.

The unitary board is endorsed by the Hampel Report as also offering:

- flexibility and speed of action; and

- the ability to delegate specific tasks effectively to sub-committees, e.g. audit, remuneration and nomination committees.

Meetings of the board

The board needs to meet regularly and reasonably often.

The composition of the board: executives and non-executives

Board balance is best achieved by a mix of executive and non-executive directors. This brings together a matrix of several inputs:

(a) on-the-ground judgement of the executive director(s);

(b) the business abilities of the non-executives (see below, page 65); and

(c) the board leadership provided by the CEO/chair.

Communication to the board

Supply of information to the board needs to be achieved promptly with the information in an appropriate:

- form; and
- quality to allow the board to do its job properly (i.e. to manage and govern).

Communication by the board

The board's specific communication and general public relations function is a pervasive area of corporate governance. The board needs to be clear, precise and motivated by maximising shareholder return (i.e. acting in the 'best interests of the company'), subject to the framework of corporate governance and legal listing, and other requirements. For more discussion of these issues, see the case studies in Chapter 18.

Measuring board performance

This was noted by the Hampel Report as something that happens on a formal basis in the USA and takes place in some UK companies. The Hampel Report called it an 'interesting development' and went on to say:

> boards might usefully consider it in the interest of continuous improvement, though we do not feel able at this stage to make a firm recommendation on the subject.[7]

This appears to be a 'watch this space' issue which may well become a firm recommendation at some stage in the future.

Arguments against measuring board performance

Boards, of course, can argue that they are already subject to fairly continuous performance monitoring by various rigorous, informed and highly motivated parties including:

- the customers;
- the shareholders and employees;
- the auditors; and
- the company's competitors;

and that to impose another round (essentially a fifth layer) of formal performance criteria would:

- be very difficult to standardise;
- divert attention away from more important and pressing company business;
- involve many attendant hours of directors and management in form-filling and 'box-ticking' (the 'box-ticking' approach to governance is specifically disapproved of by the Hampel Report – see Chapter 3); and
- be superfluous in light of the several, historically proven and standardised layers of 'informal' performance criteria (market share, results, audit, AGM, success or failure!, and so on), which have been refined over the course of very many years.

Corporate governance issues for the board *vis-à-vis* a specific director

Here we take a 'time-line' approach to the issues affecting an individual director:

- matters relevant to a director's appointment to office;
- matters likely to arise during a director's term of office; and
- matters arising on a director's departure from office.

Appointments of directors to the board

The process must be transparent, clear and fair.

Attributes of directors

Directors should meet, amongst other criteria, the following:

- be properly informed of the company's core business and strategy;
- be people of the right calibre; and
- be people who can bring openness, thoroughness and objectivity to bear on the carrying out of their roles (page 14, Hampel Report).

Training of directors

The Hampel Report recommends that a first-time director (especially of a listed company) should receive some form of training inducting them into the role. The provision of appropriate training to meet the particular company's needs is the responsibility of the board.[8]

The Institute of Directors runs several courses through its Centre for Director Development. These include intensive one- and two-day courses as well as distance learning options. There are courses on the following topics:

- the role of company director;
- the role of managing director in the small and medium-sized business;
- the role of company secretary;
- the role of company chairman;
- the role of non-executive director;
- the role of the finance director;
- finance and non-financial directors;
- funding business growth – exploring the alternatives;
- buying and selling companies;
- a director's introduction to the City;
- keys to personal effectiveness;
- business presentations and public speaking;
- strategic business direction;
- dynamic business leadership;
- developing sale strategies.

The Institute of Directors also provides courses such as the masters in corporate direction (or a diploma in company direction), which are endorsed by the Institute of Directors and put on by various UK universities.

Directors' remuneration

As we saw in Chapter 2, the controversy surrounding the size of directors' pay packages and the lack of sensitivity perceived in relation to employees and shareholders were key motivations behind the Greenbury Report, and remain highly sensitive corporate governance issues.

Disclosure of the package details

As we pointed out in Chapter 3, the Greenbury Report requires listed companies to disclose the breakdown of the component parts of the package in detail. The Greenbury Report's illustrative disclosure formats deal separately with:

(a) remuneration; and

(b) share options and other long-term incentives.

There are separate inclusions for:

- salary and fees;
- benefits;
- annual bonus;
- other amounts;
- the total for the year;
- the prior year total;
- long-term incentives for the current and previous year;
- pensions for the current and previous year.

These requirements are in addition to the Companies Act 1985 requirements requesting the aggregate of board emoluments to be disclosed in any event.

Simplification

The Hampel Report has concluded that the remuneration disclosure requirements have become 'too complicated'. It goes on to say that it would welcome simplification of the process.[9]

Remuneration committees

Boards should have remuneration committees made up of independent non-executives. The role of the remuneration committee is to:

(a) develop policy on remuneration; and

(b) devise remuneration packages for individual directors.[10]

Caution is urged in the use of intercompany comparisons when setting the amount and mix of remuneration packages.

Re-election of directors

Each director should be put up for re-election every three years or less, i.e. directors should not be 'quarantined' from the shareholders by long-term service contracts.

(The listing rules require directors of listed companies to submit themselves for re-election at their first AGM.)

Performance testing of directors

Just as with the formal measuring of board performance, this is not yet a requirement for individual directors, but has been flagged by the Hampel Report as a matter to keep an eye on in the future.[11]

Resignation from office

The shareholders should be entitled to know the reason for a director resigning:

(a) if for personal reasons, the director's privacy should be respected;

(b) if for policy, competence or other reasons, it may be wise for the board to communicate this in an apt manner.

Any payments made in respect of the early departure of a director should be handled carefully and made fully transparent (and in accordance with s.312 of the Companies Act 1985, approved by the shareholders if they involve other than service agreement amounts).

Non-executive directors

The three corporate governance reports recognise the crucial corporate governance role played by non-executive directors, whilst at the same time acknowledging that many smaller companies will not be able to meet the guidelines. Flexibility, therefore, in relation to an individual company's circumstances, is recommended by the Hampel Report.[12]

Chapter 5 deals with the non-executive director's role in corporate governance more thoroughly than here. What is intended here is to place the non-executive directors within the broader ambit of the board's general corporate governance role.

The general role of non-executive directors

Their general role is to bring an outside perspective (objectivity) to the board's deliberations and to encourage vigorous debate on policy, etc.

They have both a strategic and a monitoring function.

Objective skills criteria

The sort of matters referred to in the Hampel Report which a non-executive director may bring to the company include:

- executive experience in other companies;
- technical knowledge;
- overseas markets; and
- political contacts.

The Hampel Report makes it clear, however, that business efficacy is the yardstick for appointment when it says:

> We do not favour diversity for its own sake, to give a politically correct appearance to the list of board members or represent stakeholders.[13]

Independence

A majority of the non-executive directors should, as the Cadbury Code recommended (and is endorsed by the Hampel Committee), be:

> independent of management and free from any business or other relationship which could materially interfere with the exercise of their independent judgement.[14]

Independence can generally be ensured by the following criteria in relation to non-executive directors:

(a) their objective view of the business is maintained in that they attend board meetings on an occasional basis;

(b) they bring with them rigorous outside points of view;

(c) they are prepared to question executive management, the CEO and others when they feel it necessary;

(d) they have an appointed leader; and

(e) their fee steers clear of including bonus shares as part of the package. The Hampel Report states 'we see no objection to paying a non-executive director's remuneration in the company's shares, but do not recommend this as universal practice'.[15]

Generally

Board sensitivity is required so as to maintain both the appearance and reality of non-executive independence.

Compliance strategies for the board

The keys to corporate governance compliance for the board are as follows:

Regular meetings

The board should meet 'regularly'.

Obviously, this will depend on a number of factors, including:

(a) company's objects – the nature of the company's business; is it, for example, a simple business or a conglomerate comprising disparate activities?

(b) board numbers – how easy or necessary is it to get together as a board?

(c) quorum – what is the quorum required to carry out company business?; and

(d) delegation – how much of the board's work is devolved to the MD or chairman?

Controlling the company

The board should retain full control of the company – both in fact and by appearance.

Again, there will be several factors involved, including:

(a) to whom does the board delegate?;

(b) what are the limits of the authority which the board has delegated away? For example, the auditors will be charged with the company audit subject to supervision by the board or its finance director or a finance sub-committee.

A particular issue here is that people behind the scenes cannot be in a position where they effectively run the company in place of the board, i.e. *de facto* management. An example is the person who pulls the strings behind the scenes, and management obeys those commands, but the person is not shown on the Companies House register as a director. Such people are known as 'shadow directors' and they are treated by the courts as if they were publicly appointed directors.

Monitoring the executive

The board should remain in a position where it can monitor executive management effectively.

An example is where the hands-on, day-to-day management vests in, say, an MD, and the rest of the board is composed of non-executives, whose involvement in the company is to attend the occasional board meeting. This is the sort of scenario that certain high-profile, former government minister, non-executive directors have pleaded from time to time in recent years, in relation to key negotiations and business matters discussed at board meetings. The 'I wasn't present, I wasn't up to date, I wasn't informed' arguments will cut less and less ice. And it is no good for the MD, as this type of arrangement is putting too much emphasis on the MD always getting right the extent to which he keeps the rest of the board informed of company business.

The roles of chairman and chief executive

Separation of top jobs

Ideally, the CEO and chair roles should be filled by different people and not be unified. This is not a hard and fast rule, however, and should be judged on a company-by-company basis.[16]

The dangers of unifying the roles are graphically illustrated by the fiasco of the Robert Maxwell case where the company was essentially run as a personal fiefdom where his word was absolute and nobody, including his own family members and fellow directors, could question him. This 'patriarchal model' ('patriarchal' literally meaning 'law of the father' – apt in the Maxwell case, given the evidence produced by Kevin and Ian Maxwell and other board members) should be avoided and the best first step is to appoint independent individuals to the two posts.

Independent group(s) on the board

Where the roles of chairman and chief executive are not separate, an independent group should exist on the board with its own leader.

Board meeting agendas

A formal schedule should be followed at board meetings.

Boardroom template for corporate governance

- As the Hampel Report states, the single overriding objective is the preservation and the greatest practicable enhancement, over time, of their shareholders' investment[17]

- Other criteria of board action include the ability to:

  (a) develop and maintain sound working relationships with the company's stakeholders;

  (b) receive information from others which is timely, coherent, and accurate;

  (c) communicate to others (both within and outside the company) in a timely, coherent and honest manner; and

  (d) anticipate the possible PR fallout of board deliberations and generally to think ahead and factor in potential problems.

Notes

1 Vidal, J. (1997) *McLibel* – see bibliography.

2 *Re City Equitable Fire Insurance Co. Ltd* 1925, Ch. 407.

3 Sparrow, A. (1997) *The Responsibilities of Company Directors*, published by FT Management – see bibliography.

4 Hampel Report, page 10.

5 Hampel Report, page 16.

6 Hampel Report, page 16.
7 Hampel Report, page 27.
8 Hampel Report, page 24.
9 Hampel Report, page 61.
10 Hampel Report, page 60.
11 Hampel Report, page 27.
12 Hampel Report, page 26.
13 Hampel Report, page 27.
14 Cadbury Report, 4.12 and Hampel Report, page 25.
15 Hampel Report, page 60.
16 Hampel Report, page 28.
17 Hampel Report, page 17.

5

Particular board issues: non-executive directors

Overview   61

The general role of the non-executive directors in relation to board functions   61

Non-executives and board sub-committees   62

The importance of the independence of non-executive directors   64

The key indicators of independence of the non-executives   64

Overplaying the monitoring role   66

Independence and compliance statements   66

Non-executives and smaller companies   67

Non-executive directors' template   67

Overview

This chapter and several of the following chapters deal with specific issues of concern for a board in relation to corporate governance strategy.

These issues are as follows:

- the role of non-executive directors in the corporate governance matrix (dealt with in this chapter);
- the role played by the various corporate governance sub-committees of the board (dealt with in Chapter 6);
- internal control (i.e. within the company) (dealt with in Chapter 7);
- the requirements surrounding corporate governance compliance statements (this is discussed in Chapter 8); and
- the question of ethics and developing ethical codes (dealt with in Chapter 9).

Chapter 4, page 52 introduced some of the issues concerning non-executive directors within the broader ambit of the board's corporate governance function. This chapter expands on those broad principles.

The general role of the non-executive directors in relation to board functions

As we have seen elsewhere, the UK-style unitary board is supposed to fulfil two functions: that of management and that of governance or control.

A key criterion in fulfilling the requirements of corporate governance compliance is that the board is accountable, through disclosure, to the shareholders. The role of a non-executive director is particularly important in seeing that the executives do carry out these control, accountability and disclosure roles, as well as the management and profit-making roles. Hence the need for non-executive directors to be independent of the executive wherever possible and to be able to bring rigorous, 'outside' views to the workings of the board.

Minimising the risk for non-executive directors

For the board of directors in general, and non-executive directors in particular, there are some very simple steps they can take in order to minimise their risks. These include:

- possessing a working knowledge of their legal responsibilities, including the specific areas in which the company conducts its business;

- keeping up to date with director-specific publications, which should always be read in conjunction with specific legal advice which the board has obtained in relation to its particular circumstances;

- doing their homework – this involves reading the papers and documentation that is sent to them, and, if the information is insufficient or unclear, asking for more information;

- playing an acting role in board meetings, expressing opinions and questioning matters when they are unclear or not fully conversant with what is being discussed; and

- keeping copies of their board papers and any notes they have made and retaining a written record of their opinions. This is especially important when they disagree with the majority decision on a contentious subject, or when there is a clear difference of opinion between the non-executive members and the executive members of the board.

Non-executives and board sub-committees

The governance role of the non-executives has been increased by the three corporate governance reports, particularly with reference to the audit and directors' remuneration committees where non-executive membership should be strong (if not unanimous). Non-executive involvement is also recommended on the committee which nominates the directors. Each of these three sub-committees of the board is dealt with in more detail in Chapter 6. A brief summary of their role, as far as the non-executive directors are concerned, follows.

Non-executives and the nomination committee

The Cadbury Report at paragraph 4.30 floated the idea of boards having appointment sub-committees 'with the responsibility of proposing to the board, in the first instance, any new appointments', i.e. their role would be to recommend a shortlist and to simplify the appointment process for the full board. The Cadbury Report recommended that the nomination committee should have a majority of non-executive directors on it, and be chaired either by the chairman of the full board or by a non-executive director.

The Hampel Report at paragraph 3.19 supports 'the Cadbury committee's endorsement of the nomination committee' and goes on to say: 'indeed, we believe that the use of such a committee should be accepted as best practice, with the proviso that smaller boards may prefer to fulfil the function themselves'.

The emerging trend, therefore, in relation to nomination committees, is that their use will become more prevalent and it may well be that the next round of corporate governance investigations concludes that such a committee should become compulsory, certainly for listed companies. This trend matches the general trend for corporate governance to go through the various stages: recommendation, best practice, formalisation and enforcement.

Non-executives and the directors' remuneration committee

The Greenbury Report at paragraph 4.8 states that the remuneration committee should consist exclusively of non-executive directors with relevant experience who:

(a) have no personal financial interest, other than as shareholders, in the committee's decisions;

(b) have no 'cross-directorships' with the executive directors which could be thought to offer scope for mutual agreements to bid up each other's remuneration;

(c) have a good knowledge of the company and its executive directors, a keen interest in its progress and a full understanding of shareholders' concerns; and

(d) have a good understanding, enhanced as necessary by appropriate training or access to expert advice, of the areas of remuneration committee business.

Non-executives and the audit committee

Paragraphs 4.33 to 4.39 inclusive of the Cadbury Report on the financial aspects of corporate governance recommended that all listed companies should establish an audit committee composed of a minimum of three members of the board, that membership should be confined to the non-executive directors, and that the majority of those non-executives on the audit committee should be independent.

The importance of the independence of non-executive directors

The Cadbury Report spoke of the 'essential quality' (paragraph 4.12) which non-executive directors should bring to the board's deliberations as being that of 'independence of judgement'.

The independence of non-executive directors is becoming more crucial in terms of a company's public relations performance and in terms of the company's corporate governance strategy. The general trend appears to be that best practice recommendations will gradually become legally enforceable requirements.

The key indicators of independence of the non-executives

Cadbury went on to recommend that the majority of non-executives on a board should be independent of the company. 'Independence' includes reference to the following matters.

Fees

- Non-executive directors should be paid by way of fees and shareholdings.
- Cadbury makes it clear that, in the light of the 'significant' demands being made on non-executive directors, their fees should reflect the time they devote to the company's affairs.
- There is justification to pay additional fees in relation to matters such as chairing board committees (appointment, remuneration or audit, for example).

Shares

- Cadbury makes it clear that, in order to safeguard their independence, non-executive directors should not, as a matter of 'great practice', participate in share option schemes; nor should their services be pensionable.
- Apart from their fees and shareholdings, non-executive directors should be independent of management.
- Ideally, non-executives should be paid in a way that is independent of the performance of the organisation, i.e. they should not receive bonus payments for greater profits; nor should they participate in bonus share schemes.

- They should be free from any business or other relationship which could materially interfere with the exercise of their independent judgement.

The Cadbury Report then left it up to the board of each company, in any particular case, to decide that these broad parameters as to the independence of non-executive directors had been met. The details as to independence should then be disclosed in the directors' report forming part of the company's annual return.

The above discussion points to the fact that the monitoring role of the non-executives is probably more crucial than their secondary role of acting alongside, and with, the management.

This dual role of the non-executives is likely to continue, given the Hampel Report's rejection of the continental-style two-tier board in which non-executives would serve solely on a supervisory board without any formal executive responsibilities. The unitary boards are seen as more appropriate to UK business in that they allow a more dynamic relationship between the executive and non-executive segments of the board, and manage to resolve the potential conflict between the management and monitoring roles.

Business interests and links

- Non-executives should be independent, with no business or financial interests in the company.

Independent judgement

- They should be able to bring independent judgement to bear on issues of board strategy, company performance, the use of resources, the making of key appointments, and standards of conduct.

Business relationships

- Hampel agrees with Cadbury that the non-executive director should be independent and, adopting the wording of Cadbury:

> free from any business or other relationship which could materially interfere with the exercise of their independent judgement [whilst Hampel agrees with that definition, the report goes on to say] after careful consideration we do not consider that it is practicable to lay down more precise criteria for independence. We agree with Cadbury that it should be for the board to take a view on whether an individual director is independent in the above sense (page 25, Hampel Final Report).

The Hampel Report therefore deliberately steers clear of setting out a checklist of the sort of matters which go further than Cadbury and ensure independence. Those further criteria would be matters such as the following (mentioned above on page 64):

- non-executive directors have not been previously employed. This is taken as 5 years in an executive capacity by the company;

- they (or businesses in which they have an interest) are not in a supplier or customer relationship with the company of which they are a non-executive director.

Overplaying the monitoring role

At paragraph 3.7 of the Hampel Report, the report states that there has been 'an unintended side effect' after the Cadbury Report raised the profile of the non-executive director and that this has been to overemphasise the monitoring role, i.e. the control of the executive role. Hampel therefore, in broad terms, is putting the discretion for non-executive independence back in the hands of the board, and this approach ties in with the tailor-made attitude towards corporate governance which the company should have, rather than the box-ticking approach.

Justifying independence

The Hampel Report justifies the approach set out above by providing that, of course, the boards will disclose in their annual reports the basis of non-executive independence and should be able to justify their views if challenged.

Hampel goes on to say that non-executive directors who are not strictly independent may none the less 'make a useful contribution to the board'.

Independence and compliance statements

These conclusions of the Hampel Report correspond with the attitude prescribed for the board in terms of its compliance statements. Where there are compliance problems, just as where there are possible problems as to non-executives not being independent, the board should speak with one voice and should have a thorough explanation strategy in place promptly.

Non-executives and smaller companies

The Hampel Report at paragraph 3.8 talks of the valuable expertise which non-executive directors can bring to management, especially in small companies. In this sense, they can act as mentors to relatively inexperienced executives. Hampel goes on to state: 'what matters in every case is that the non-executive director should command the respect of the executives and should be able to work with them in a cohesive team to further the company's interest'.

Non-executive directors' template

A summary of the key issues concerning non-executive directors within the corporate governance matrix is as follows.

- Non-executive directors are seen as vital to emerging corporate governance practice.

- Wherever possible, non-executive directors should be independent of the business and able to cast a critical eye over the workings of the executive board.

- Non-executive directors are crucial in terms of any of the sub-committees of the board – for example, the appointment and remuneration of directors and the audit committee.

- Such sub-committees should be largely composed of non-executive directors and, wherever appropriate, non-executive directors should chair such sub-committees.

- The question of 'independence' needs to be monitored on a regular basis in relation to non-executive directors.

- The Hampel Report recognises the commercial reality that true 'independence' may not be achievable in terms of the non-executive directors, especially for smaller companies.

- Small companies which do not have non-executive directors on the board should consider appointing them as a matter of good practice – obviously, this will be important if the company grows and/or lists; it is also in line with the corporate governance trends, which are increasingly promoting the importance of, and role played by, non-executive directors.

6

Particular board issues: the sub-committees on directors' appointments, pay and the audit

Overview   71

The nomination of directors' committee   71

The remuneration committee   73

The audit committee   75

Template for the board sub-committees   76

Overview

The introduction of corporate governance procedures and requirements in the 1990s has seen the advent of three particular sub-committees of the board of directors. These committees deal with the appointment of directors, setting directors' pay and dealing with the company's auditors.

The purpose of this chapter is to consider briefly the work of each of these three sub-committees.

The nomination of directors' committee

Background

There is a growing trend towards companies appointing nomination committees. The general rule of developing corporate governance practice seems to be that the larger the company, the more likely it is to have a nomination committee. It is not compulsory for a company to have a nomination committee, but the Cadbury Committee and the Hampel Report endorse the use of such a committee as best practice. The Hampel Report at paragraph 3.19 adds the proviso that smaller companies may wish to fulfil the functions of the nomination committee themselves. There is therefore flexibility in relation to the nomination committees, but generally the trend is towards having them and allowing for more transparency in relation to board nominations.

The role of a nomination committee

The nomination committee is strictly speaking a sub-committee of the main board and therefore does not have executive powers. Its focus is the nomination of potential directors to the board and the work of the nomination committee revolves around helping to ensure:

- that the search for new directors is thorough;
- that the nomination process proceeds at a steady pace without being delayed unreasonably; and
- that appointments to the board are made on the basis of merit against an objective and agreed written set of criteria setting out the job specifications.

Composition of the nomination committee

The nomination committee will usually be chaired by the chairman of the board and the rest of the nomination committee should be composed of independent non-executive directors. One of the executive directors may also be on the nomination committee. Obviously, the committee does not want to be too large, otherwise it becomes unwieldy as a sub-committee reporting to the board.

The recruitment process

The recruitment process in selecting a director to join the board, on a time-line basis, would proceed as follows.

Drawing up the job specification

The nomination committee would be charged with preparing a written job specification, which should set out the criteria which a candidate would need to fulfil and provide reference to personal details such as age and particular experience.

The job specification should also detail particular matters, work experience, or work in certain industries, etc. which would make it inappropriate for a particular candidate to apply for the position. For example, there may be competing industry or trade secret problems.

The job specification should set out the nature of the role and responsibilities and duties that go with such a role in as much detail as is appropriate and commercially prudent.

Meeting the candidates

The nomination committee may 'vet' the candidates and prepare a shortlist to be interviewed by the full board. Whatever process is adopted, it should be transparent and should both be 'seen' to, and should, shortlist or select candidates consistent with the written criteria. The nomination committee can therefore provide a useful 'filter' by saving time for the board and reporting findings back to the board ahead of the actual appointment decision.

Making the appointment

The appointment of a new member of the board should be made after a candidate has had an opportunity to meet all members of the board and after a discussion and decision-making process has taken place involving the full board. This stage should reiterate the transparency and thoroughness of the process.

The appointment letter

A thorough letter setting out the terms of the appointment, the nature of the tasks and responsibilities of the director, and other pertinent details, should be sent to the director promptly. Obviously, it is also important that the new director becomes quickly and efficiently acquainted with all aspects of the business. This aspect should not be underestimated with non-executive directors. It is also important for new directors to be advised as to the terms of any insurance cover they will receive in their capacity as directors. Such cover will not extend to liabilities arising out of negligence, default or breach of duty or trust by a director, and so the exact terms and limits of any proposed policy should be sorted out quickly.

The remuneration committee

Background

Directors' pay and the role of remuneration committees was the primary focus of the Greenbury Report in response to public concern about the levels of pay being awarded to directors 'by themselves', i.e. there was certainly a perception of a conflict of interest, as well as a perception of greed.

The Greenbury (and the Cadbury) Report recommended that the boards of listed companies should establish a remuneration committee to develop policies on the pay awarded to executive directors and other senior executives of the company.

The Hampel Committee is in broad agreement with this proposal.

Following the Greenbury Report, the Stock Exchange Listing Rules implemented several of the Greenbury recommended actions and section 12.43(x) of the Listing Rules requires companies to include in their annual report:

(a) a report by the remuneration committee on behalf of the board, focusing on the company's remuneration policy for executive directors; and

(b) details of the remuneration packages of each director.

The role of the remuneration committee

As with the appointment sub-committee, the remuneration committee is a sub-committee which is responsible to, and reports to, the main board of directors. Its role is to distance those who set pay levels *for* the executive *from* the executive. This is to guard against a basic conflict of interest and a public relations problem (at least potentially) for the board.

There is therefore a dual role for the remuneration committee: to set broad policy requirements for the company as to remuneration, and to set specific packages for individual directors.

Composition of the remuneration committee

All three corporate governance reports have recommended the establishment of remuneration committees as good practice and Greenbury and Hampel have recommended that the membership of the remuneration committee should be made up wholly of independent non-executive directors. It is recognised, however, that executive directors may need to attend for appropriate matters of business.

The bottom line is that executive directors should not be (or be seen to be) deciding their own remuneration.

The remuneration process for directors

The Hampel Report comments on the fairly poor standard of reporting by companies under section 12.43(x) of the Listing Rules in relation to remuneration policy in company annual reports. It recommends that companies should avoid generic, anodyne references such as the need to 'recruit, retain and motivate' or to pay 'market rates'. The Hampel Report recommends that companies should, in reporting on directors' pay:

(a) set their own circumstances in context;

(b) provide more detailed information; and

(c) draw attention to factors specific to the company.

The Hampel Report makes some criticism of the amount of detail in relation to remuneration disclosures required by the Listing Rules. The Hampel Report makes it clear that it wishes for such disclosure requirements to be simplified. This would, it argues, reduce the administrative burden on the company as well as make such information more readily accessible to shareholders and 'lay readers'.

Pensions disclosure

The Greenbury Report also recommends that the financial implications of pension payments to directors by the company should be set out, and this has been put into effect by the London Stock Exchange in amending the Listing Rules. The Hampel Report specifically recommends (at paragraph 4.19) that companies spell out that pension transfer values represent a liability of the company (and that such transfer values cannot meaningfully be added to a director's annual remuneration).

The audit committee

Background

The third sub-committee reporting to the board is the audit committee. The background to such committees lies in the growth in the number and complexity of financial matters of which the board needs to be apprised, and in the increasing flow of specialist financial communication between the board and the external auditors. The audit committee, as a specialist sub-committee, is able to focus on such matters.

Role of the audit committee

As discussed above, the audit committee's primary rationale is to focus on financial matters and on the relationship between the auditors and the board, and to report to the board.

Composition of the audit sub-committee

The audit committee should consist of at least three non-executive directors, at least two of whom are 'independent' (for information on independence, see Chapter 5). The Hampel Report at paragraph 48 states that it does not favour a general relaxation for smaller companies, but at the same time recommends that flexibility be shown by smaller companies, and that they consider their own circumstances in relation to establishing such a committee and its composition.

The processes of the audit sub-committee

The role of the audit committee is to keep a watching brief on the objectivity of the auditors and on questions of value for money in the relationship between the company and the auditors.

The audit sub-committee is designed to achieve better and more effective dialogue between the board and the auditors, and to act as a conduit for 'best practice' to evolve.

For those companies which do not have an audit sub-committee, they should, from time to time, review the need for one.

Template for the board sub-committees

The following matters should be considered in relation to the board sub-committees.

- The three main board sub-committees are those dealing with the appointment and pay of directors and the audit.

- Such sub-committees have a reporting role rather than an executive role, i.e. they report to the full board.

- The rationale for such sub-committees is that they streamline the work of the board and make decision-making processes more efficient.

- Such sub-committees should be composed of a majority of non-executive directors.

- Such non-executive directors should be 'independent' as per the requirements of Chapter 5.

- Such sub-committees have an important public relations role to play in terms of corporate governance compliance. They exist to make communication more efficient and transparent.

7

Particular board issues: internal control

Overview 79

General points as to internal control 79

Risk management 80

Template for internal control 80

Overview

The concept of internal control in terms of corporate governance was introduced by the Cadbury Report which recommended (Cadbury Code, paragraph 4.5) that 'the directors should report on the effectiveness of the company's system of internal control' and that this report should be reviewed by the auditors.

Determining the exact extent of 'internal control' is not easy, and the concept has come to embrace the following matters:

- the safeguarding of company assets;
- the maintenance of proper accounting records;
- the reliability of financial information used within the company or for publication to third parties; and
- controls to ensure effective and efficient operations and compliance with laws and regulations generally.

The Hampel Report provides that directors and management should consider all aspects of control, and should not artificially separate 'financial control' from other controls. In broad terms, therefore, the board should maintain and review control systems which address all elements of internal control whether financial or otherwise.

At paragraph 6.13, the Hampel Committee essentially replicates the Cadbury control concerns by listing the following matters as coming under the 'control' umbrella:

- business risk assessment and response;
- financial management;
- compliance with laws and regulations;
- safeguarding of assets, including the minimising of fraud or the risk of fraud.

The Hampel Report leaves it open as to whether companies set up an internal audit function.

General points as to internal control

- Companies need to pay attention to their *own circumstances* in setting up internal control and commenting on such internal control.
- Companies do not need to have internal audit functions, but should review such a possibility, based on their own needs.

- Corrective procedures need to be put in place as part of internal control. For example, if there has been fraud, or problems with the audit, how can these be overcome and consigned to 'one offs' rather than becoming possibly 'systematic'? The internal control function should be constantly seeking areas of improvement in terms of the control mechanisms.
- Control mechanisms need to pick up potential problems promptly.
- The control environment needs to be driven top-down by the board, so that it filters though the company from senior management through to all employees. Proper delegation and accountability is a key part of this, as is distributing clear information and communicating effectively with staff and others.

Risk management

- Companies need to consider their own particular risk management methods and strategies. It may even be worth having a risk committee. Such risks may be financial, but they will not necessarily be limited to financial matters.
- A risk committee can work closely with insurance underwriters and others in reviewing and monitoring current policies of insurance and minimising insurance risk.
- At the end of the day, it is the board of directors who have overall responsibility for the company's system of internal financial and other control. The board needs to achieve control through efficient organisation, resourcing and delegation.

Template for internal control

Those matters which are relevant to a company's internal control mechanisms and its corporate governance performance include the following.

- Internal control is not limited to financial matters.
- Internal control is the ultimate responsibility of the board of directors.
- Internal control policy and implementation should be 'top-down' and properly communicated to all members of the company.
- Internal control needs to be put in place promptly and certainly well before year-end. It is ongoing.
- Particular problems need to be spotted early and pro-active solutions adopted.

- Companies should learn from their own histories and mistakes and should bear them in mind at all times in terms of effective internal control.

- A central register of internal control matters should be maintained within the company, i.e. the 'paper' can then be kept in one place and one person can monitor it for the board.

- As part of adopting their own strategies, companies should pursue information technology solutions available on the market. Obviously, this is a rapidly moving market, especially as the so-called 'millennium bug' problem looms.

- Companies should consider whether or not they need an internal audit to be carried out and whether they should have an audit sub-committee reporting to the board (see Chapter 6).

8

Particular board issues: compliance statements

Overview 85

The scope of compliance statements 86

Compliance and the Cadbury *Code of Best Practice* 86

Types of Cadbury compliance statements 86

The Greenbury Report and compliance 87

The Hampel Report and compliance 89

Compliance strategies for the board 90

Compliance statements template 91

Overview

Statements of compliance are brief statements set out in a company's annual reports (either in the directors' report, or in the accounts, or both), essentially providing a statement to the effect that the company has complied with either its general, or specific, corporate governance requirements.

Each of the three corporate governance reports to date has referred to a compliance requirement. The Cadbury Report at paragraph 1.3 referred to the fact that the London Stock Exchange would require compliance statements in relation to the Cadbury *Code of Best Practice* (and such statements would also need to give reasons for any areas of non-compliance).

Similarly, the Greenbury Report at paragraph 1.18 provided that listed companies registered in the UK should comply with the *Code of Best Practice* and report annually to shareholders about compliance with it.

The Hampel Report at paragraph 1.23 noted that it would pass the combined set of principles set out in the Cadbury, Greenbury and Hampel Reports to the London Stock Exchange, so that the completed document could sit alongside the Listing Rules. The Hampel Report leaves it open as to changes to be made by the London Stock Exchange, and goes on to note: 'this committee certainly envisages that the current requirement for companies to confirm or otherwise comply with Cadbury will be superseded by a requirement to make a statement to show how they:

(a) apply the principles; and

(b) comply with the combined code and, in the latter case, to justify any significant variances.' (Hampel Report, paragraph 1.23)

It is obvious from this statement in the Hampel Report that the issue of compliance will become ever more important in terms of corporate governance developments.

Environmental risk management (and accompanying environmental statements) is a growing trend in the corporate governance field. Environmental issues are specifically dealt with in Chapter 16.

The scope of compliance statements

A company wishing to guarantee that it has exceeded the compliance requirement of the *Code of Best Practice* or another corporate governance document could become involved in a limitless amount of administration. From a practical point of view, therefore, it is advisable to restrict the statement to the Cadbury *Code of Best Practice*, the Greenbury directors' remuneration matters, and other particular areas. If statements are to be extended beyond the *Code of Best Practice*, the practical position for companies will be to wait for the consolidation of the three corporate governance reports to be undertaken by the Hampel Committee. However, the broader the requirements beyond the *Code of Best Practice* and Greenbury, the more difficult it will be for any company to issue a blanket statement of compliance, and it will no doubt deter smaller companies from full compliance.

Compliance and the Cadbury Code of Best Practice

As noted at the outset of this chapter, the compliance notion began with the Cadbury *Code of Best Practice*. In terms of this code, the compliance requirement is that the company provides a statement to the effect that the company has complied with the Cadbury *Code of Best Practice*. Cadbury also imposes the requirement that areas of non-compliance with the *Code of Best Practice* are noted, as well as reasons for non-compliance.

Types of Cadbury compliance statements

There are several types of compliance statements which have emerged as a result of Cadbury, including the following.

Full compliance

This is a blanket statement providing that the company has reviewed its procedures in terms of the Cadbury *Code of Best Practice* and, in the directors' opinion, the company fully complies at the time of the annual report and has done so throughout the 12 months preceding the annual report.

Highlight key issues

A second format provides a general statement to the effect that the company has complied with the *Code of Best Practice* throughout the year and highlights particular matters or points of compliance, for example, that the board has met regularly; that there is separation between the positions of chairman and chief executive, and that the non-executive directors are independent of the board.

This type of compliance statement, whilst not strictly necessary, may seek to provide good publicity for the company in terms of its 'good corporate citizen' ethos in respect of its shareholders and potential shareholders. Therefore, from a public relations point of view, it may make good sense.

Explain particular issues of non-compliance

A third form of compliance statement would state that the company has met the provisions of the *Code of Best Practice* in all respects except in relation to specific exceptions. For example, it may well be that a non-executive director is not, in fact, independent of the board. For example, a non-executive director may also be a director or a shareholder in the company, or a non-executive director may be associated with professional advisers to the company.

Form and content of compliance statements

The form and content of the compliance statement are not prescribed; therefore a company should adopt the form of compliance statement which best suits its needs.

As mentioned elsewhere, every company should avoid the 'box-ticking' approach, specifically referred to as being inappropriate by the Hampel Final Report.

The place of the compliance statement

Again this is not prescriptive, but it will usually be incorporated in the directors' report or as part of a separate statement on corporate governance.

The Greenbury Report and compliance

The compliance statement in relation to directors' remuneration is required as part of the London Stock Exchange Listing Rules. This is for all accounting periods beginning on, or after, 31 December 1995. Such statements run to between two and approximately twelve pages in length. Statements go into policy considerations on directors' remuneration, comparing current year with previous year and trans-effective remuneration. The length and type of service agreement for directors would generally be discussed, and particular issues of importance should be highlighted. The directors' emoluments should be broken down into the following categories:

- salary;
- performance-related annual bonus;
- performance-related longer than 1 year bonus;
- other bonus payments;
- taxable benefits;
- current year total;
- previous year total.

The amounts should be listed for each individual director and should include reference to executive director and non-executive director.

The taxable benefits will include such items as:

- car expenses;
- medical expenses;
- relocation expenses;
- subsidised mortgage payments.

Pensions policy should also be explained and documented, and reference should be made to the following items:

- contributions to pensions from individual directors during the current year;
- increase in the pension entitlements accrued during the current year;
- transfer value of the increase in accrued pension during the current year;
- total accrued pension as at the year's end;
- total accrued pension as at previous year's end.

Details of shares held, and share options, should also be included as part of the Greenbury disclosure and in respect of compliance provisions.

The Hampel Report and compliance

The Hampel Report provides that companies should include in their annual report and accounts a 'narrative statement' of how they apply the relevant principles of corporate governance to their particular circumstances. This obviously ties in with the prevailing ethos that corporate governance should be company specific and tailored to particular circumstances. Such a statement could, the Hampel Report suggests, be linked to the compliance statement required by the Listing Rules. There are 17 principles of corporate governance identified by the Hampel Report which could theoretically be discussed as part of the narrative to the compliance statement. These are as follows:

1. the board, i.e. its composition; ethos; direction;

2. the chairman and chief executive officer, i.e. are the roles split?; what is entailed in each job?;

3. board balance, i.e. between the executive and non-executive sections;

4. supply of information to the board, i.e. how and by whom; dealing with sub-committees;

5. appointment to the board, i.e. during the course of the year who was appointed to the board and by what process? In particular, what roles were played by the appointment and remuneration committees (if any)?

6. re-election, i.e. which directors' service agreements came up for renewal, and what was the process of their re-election? – was it a matter put before shareholders, or was it a matter decided on by the board?

7. directors' remuneration, i.e. what is the current year remuneration policy, and are there any major changes from previous year remuneration policy? What is anticipated for remuneration policy in the following year? Are there any particular issues of controversy or shareholder concern which need to be given preference in terms of the statement?

8. level and make-up of remuneration, i.e. what are the various components of the salary package?

9. procedure for developing policy and fixing executive remuneration, i.e. what is the role and function of the remuneration committee? What broad policy are they following? There may be reference to other industries, although the Hampel Report says that this should not be overplayed – companies should look to their own particular circumstances and be able to explain them.

10 remuneration disclosure, i.e. the matter set out in the Listing Rules as to directors' remuneration.

11 institutional shareholders' voting policy, i.e. what special issues or matters have attracted the attention of institutional shareholders?

12 dialogue between companies and investors, i.e. what mechanisms have been put in place to communicate more effectively with shareholders?

13 evaluation of governance disclosures, i.e. how do the company's particular circumstances fit in relation to the broad framework of corporate governance?

14 the AGM, i.e. what issues of policy are going to be discussed at the AGM? Which directors will be subject to shareholder approval in terms of renewal of service agreements, etc?.

15 financial reporting, i.e. what matters are there to report in relation to the audit and the end-of-year financial reports?

16 internal control, i.e. what are the internal control mechanisms and what has been the role of the audit committee (if any)?; and

17 relationships with the auditors, i.e. what other work have the auditors done for the company? Are there any issues of concern as to auditor independence?

The matters referred to above individually and collectively amount to the need for more effective and fuller communication by the board to its various stakeholders. Good communication effectively translates into good public relations strategy. The board should be as expansive as it can be.

Compliance strategies for the board

The first point is that the board should be fully up to speed on compliance and non-compliance issues. Probably the best way to do this is to produce a board paper. Where there is a possibility of non-compliance which will need to be reported, the board should discuss this as early as possible, be clear about why the company will not be able to comply, and once the non-compliance strategy has been determined, speak with one voice in relation to all stakeholders to minimise any adverse public relations ramifications. The more crucial the area of non-compliance, the greater should be the efforts made to explain why the company, in its particular circumstances, will not be complying with the *Code of Best Practice*. In general terms, as has been outlined elsewhere in this volume, public relations and controlling public relations to the company's best advantage are assuming greater prominence all the time. Refer to the first of the case studies in Chapter 18 for an example of PR in a practical context.

Compliance statements template

Amongst the matters which need to be considered in relation to compliance policy are the following.

- Particular reference needs to be made to the terms of the specific report they refer to, e.g. Cadbury, Greenbury or other.

- The requirement imposed by Cadbury is that a compliance statement must also deal with areas of non-compliance and provide reasons why compliance has not been achieved.

- For particular issues concerning Cadbury and Greenbury compliance statements, the London Stock Exchange Listing Rules should be studied.

- The Hampel Report has recommended a narrative-style compliance statement dealing with several issues.

- Compliance statements appear to be here to stay, and their importance has been stressed by all three corporate governance reports.

- It may be, in future, that there is a requirement for a 'super' compliance statement which combines issues from all three corporate governance reports.

- As with other areas of corporate governance, the board, in preparing compliance statements, needs to give special consideration to the public relations ramifications of the report's contents.

9

Particular board issues: ethics and ethical codes

Background   95

Defining ethics   95

Formalising ethics   95

The content of ethical codes   96

Making ethics work   97

Ethics template   97

Background

The corporate governance project of the 1990s has been backgrounded by ethical considerations. Inherent in such considerations is an apparent paradox: is ethical behaviour by companies consistent with companies' striving to make a profit?

Ethics are very much a part of the 1990s economic and cultural environment generally. This has been the case in relation to corporations with the publication of the three corporate governance reports within the space of six years. More broadly, ethical concerns about 'public life' (for instance, the standards applying to politicians and other public officials) have been evidenced by committees such as Nolan and Scott.

At the same time, consumer and customer awareness of ethical considerations has become heightened by more efficient communication techniques, wider use of media involvement and a greater awareness of the civic responsibility of companies and others, pushed by more active, better organised and informed individual shareholders.

Defining ethics

Any strict definition of ethics, especially in the corporate sense, is difficult to set out. There will always be shades of grey and areas of doubt. One can simply put it in fairly anodyne terms of 'not doing to others what you wouldn't wish have done to yourself'. For ethics to carry weight within a company, there need to be agreed principles within a framework which is known to all of the employees of the company, and is led from the top, i.e. by the board. Those ethics obviously also need to be practical and commercially realistic, i.e. tailor-made to the company's own projects and aims.

Formalising ethics

If ethics are to play a practical part in the company's conduct, it seems inevitable that the company needs to formalise or codify its position. In this way it then has a benchmark by which it can measure itself, monitor content and improve over given time periods. There may be two codes of ethics which work side by side: one for the board of directors and one for the company as a whole. The directors as fiduciaries owe paramount responsibilities of trust and honesty to the company, and any code of ethics would need to be seen to enhance and clarify that position for the specific needs of the particular company.

A company-wide code of ethics could be communicated to all employees and could also be communicated to customers and others. Examples of companies claiming 'ethical governance' are the Body Shop PLC and the Co-operative Bank. The irony is that, in the process of claiming the ethical high ground, companies can also become subject to closer media and customer scrutiny – witness the recent backlashes against companies such as the Body Shop in relation to its particular ethical claims.

The content of ethical codes

Nowhere in the corporate governance reports is there a requirement that there be ethical codes. It is therefore up to each company to develop them as they see fit. Some of the matters which may be appropriate to such codes would be as follows.

Directors' codes

- That directors carry out their functions honestly, diligently and in the company's best interests.
- That they are loyal at all times to the company and put the company first.
- That they would not act in any matter which would embarrass or conflict with the company.
- That they should not use confidential information for personal gain.
- That they should maintain high personal standards of conduct.

Many of these matters are covered by statutory provisions of the Companies Act 1985 and by common law as far as directors' fiduciary duties are concerned. They may also be matters of contract in so far as they form part of a director's service agreement with the company.

Employee ethical codes

Employee ethical codes may include reference to the following matters.

- That in dealing with customers, employees adopt standard and agreed 'company procedures' and do not waiver from them.
- That, apart from gifts of a nominal amount, an employee is not able to receive a gift from a customer or potential customer.

- The same considerations apply to 'entertainment' provided by customers or potential customers.
- Such an ethical code may go on to outline the company's attitude towards broader issues, such as the environment, developing countries of the world and racial discrimination. For example, the Body Shop claims that it is against animal testing within the cosmetics and toiletries industry.

Making ethics work

As the Hampel Report comments, the move towards regulation of companies has perhaps shifted too far in the 1990s, i.e. there is an argument that they are overpoliced and overmonitored. Whilst such an attitude may be the view of companies, customers, on the other hand, would probably say that the ethical movement has only just begun. The ethical paradigm has to balance several factors, including:

- the need for companies to make a profit in increasingly competitive environments;
- the need to set standards comparable to competitors in terms of ethics;
- the need to satisfy the public relations imperatives increasingly at work in the market place; and
- the maintaining and selling of ethical policies within the company by filtering them top-down from the board to all employees.

Ethics template

Among the key ethical concerns arising out of the three corporate governance reports are the following.

- Ethics form the background to the corporate governance reports, but there are no specific 'ethical' requirements, as such.
- For ethical practices to work effectively, companies need to pay attention to their particular circumstances and to try to map out ethical approaches appropriate to their needs and aspirations.
- The best way of doing this would seem to be to formalise statements of ethics and to monitor and improve such statements as and when necessary.

- Whatever the view of companies and directors, it seems that ethical concerns are here to stay and the company which is seen as ethically informed and responsible will be a long way ahead of a company characterised by customers, the public and others as ethically 'uninformed'.

10

Corporate governance for the company's auditors: general issues

The auditor's role in the company   101

The auditor's legal position   101

The role of the auditors in the corporate governance matrix   104

Auditors and their external review function   107

Auditors getting it wrong: their legal position   107

Corporate governance issues to watch out for: auditors   109

Auditors' template   110

The auditor's role in the company

The auditor's central role is to provide an objective criterion of judgement of the accuracy of the company's accounts before they go before shareholders at the annual general meeting.

The two main accounting documents are as follows.

Profit and loss statement

A statement showing a summary of the company's trading/ manufacturing and profit performance over the course of an accounting period; and

Balance sheet

A snapshot on a given day of the company's net asset, cash and liability position.

The auditor's legal position

Generally

The auditors play, as the Hampel Report puts it, a 'vital role' in the company (Hampel Report, page 49).

Independence

The auditor is required to be independent (just as are the non-executive directors) of the company and the board. The auditors are not there to rubber stamp the accounts, but to go over them closely, to question assumptions and values and to work to a general formula such as 'true and accurate' or 'true and fair'. Their overarching role is to determine, on an independent basis, an answer to the question 'are the accounts, as prepared for the company, "true and fair"' or similar?

Objective assurance

The auditors are required to provide the shareholders with 'independent and objective assurance on the reliability of the financial statements and of certain other information provided by the company'.[1]

The underlying assumption is that the auditor 'visits' the company's premises annually and does this specialist task and then disappears. The 1980s, however, changed the board–auditor relationship from this traditional arm's length one to one where the auditors were providing year-round and other services to the company. This meant that the relationship became one less than arm's length and the auditor's traditional independence was put under pressure. As a result of the 1980s phenomenon of 'cosying up' between boards and auditors, there has been a spate of litigation dealing with the issue of the auditor's professional duty in relation to getting their work done accurately (this litigation is discussed below on page 107).

For an example of auditors straying into non-traditional areas of work and getting sued, take the following recent report:

'Coopers and Lybrand, the Big Six accountancy firm, is being sued by 14 financial institutions who are debenture holders in Resort Hotels, a company which crashed four years ago and which was audited by Coopers. The plaintiffs, which include Axa Equity and Law Life Assurance, Commercial Union Life Assurance and Legal and General Assurance Society, are suing Coopers over a rights issue held two years before the company collapsed.'[2]

This piece on Coopers and Lybrand illustrates several trends concerning auditors:

(a) auditors carry out, as a baseline service, the actual audit;

(b) they also 'bolt on' other services and areas of advice, in the above case, for example, advice on a share rights issue;

(c) the auditors' clients, including traditionally conservative insurance companies, etc., are quite prepared to sue even the biggest of auditing firms these days if they perceive a case of 'carelessness'; and

(d) resort to the courts and litigation processes are ever more popular in terms of sorting out financial and other disputes involving companies in the UK (this is a trend we also comment on in Chapters 2 and 17).

The '10 per cent of business from one client' guideline

One of the matters in the professional guidance for auditors issued by their own professional body and commented on by the Hampel Report is the so-called '10 per cent rule,' i.e. where an auditor derives 10 per cent or more of their fees from just one major client.

The implication is that 10 per cent becomes a critical threshold – any more than 10 per cent means the auditor's business is too concentrated in one client and there is a risk that the auditor will actually lose, or be perceived by shareholders and others to lose, independence.

The Hampel Report recommends that the 10 per cent rule should be 'examined' by professional bodies and companies. Hampel goes on to query whether, in fact, the 10 per cent threshold should actually be reduced so as to safeguard the impression of independence.

The 10 per cent rule becomes a matter signalled by Hampel (much like performance criteria for the board, as we saw in Chapter 4) for the board to keep a 'weather eye' on. It may become the 8 per cent or even 5 per cent rule over time.

The rights of auditors

According to the Hampel Report, the vital role of auditors 'justifies the special position of the auditors under the Companies Act 1985'.[3]

Some of the 'special position' criteria or rights of the auditors are as follows:

(a) independent and objective of the company and the board: this is not only for the purpose of the preparation of financial returns and statements but for other key matters of company business (for example, with financial assistance proposed to be given by the company to a shareholder for the purchase of the company's shares);

(b) shareholders' meetings must be held in order to remove the auditor: i.e. there must be a shareholders' meeting to remove the auditors even in a company operating without a normal meetings procedure and adopting business decisions by a written solution procedure (i.e. where a potential resolution is circulated and signed by each and every member); and

(c) written resolutions – vetted first by the auditor: where a company adopts the written resolution procedure once the resolution is signed by all members, it is not fully effective until 7 days have elapsed, during which time the auditor has a chance to review the proposed resolution; and either to accept the resolution in its signed format or, alternatively, to insist that a formal shareholders' meeting is held.

The auditor's legal duties

As members of a professionally qualified and accredited body, auditors owe a 'duty of care' (literally this means a duty to be careful) of a theoretically high standard to the company (i.e. principally the shareholders). There has been considerable recent case law in the UK on the nature of the auditor's duty of care. Much of this litigation has arisen in the light of the 1980s corporate practices and the changing nature of the auditor–board relationship. It has also been part of the growing trend to litigate in the UK (which is really an influence from the USA). These UK auditor cases are still the basis of emerging principles. They are discussed below on page 107.

The role of the auditors in the corporate governance matrix

The Hampel Report makes it clear that the auditor's role is to respond to information given and to policy set by the board of directors. The auditor's roles are overseeing and monitoring; not to initiate corporate governance policy or to carry it out. These tasks remain the province of the board.

Therefore, we can say that the auditor's role in the corporate governance matrix replicates the auditor's general legal position in relation to the company.

The general corporate governance position of the auditors

Working with the board

The work done by the auditors inevitably links in with the performance of the board.

(a) Internal controls – the board

   The board is responsible for setting up and maintaining efficient financial and other internal control systems within the company.

(b) External controls – the auditors

   The auditors, as being responsible for external financial controls, build on the foundations laid down by the board. These external review functions are briefly discussed below.

Coordination and dialogue

Good financial and other control systems require the coordinated efforts of both the board and the auditors. The Hampel Report recommends that the optimum form of communication between board and auditor in relation to the company's system of internal controls be kept private; this will encourage best practice to develop.[4]

Identifying deficiencies

> If the directors fall short of high standards of corporate governance, the auditors may be able to identify the deficiency; they cannot make it good.[5]

Not an executive role in terms of corporate governance

The executive role (i.e. formulating corporate governance compliance policies and making good any corporate governance problems) falls to the board of directors, not to the auditors, whose role is one of monitoring the board and remaining at arm's length in respect of the company.

Maintaining independence

The auditors must be seen to maintain an independent working relationship with the company. This involves two separate aspects:

(a) the relationship between the company and the auditors; as we have discussed, this should be, and remain, at arm's length and independent; and

(b) within the company. This is achieved by having an audit sub-committee on the board, whose role and function is discussed below.

The audit sub-committee

The audit sub-committee is composed of members of the company board.

Recommended membership of the audit sub-committee

The recommended membership of the audit sub-committee is at least three non-executive directors (with a majority of those non-executives to be independent of management).

The Hampel Report acknowledges that smaller companies may have difficulty meeting these targets, so that each company should consider its individual circumstances on its merits.

The role of the audit sub-committee

Its role is to oversee the relationship between the board and the auditor and to check that 'independence' is maintained between the two, so as to ensure shareholder confidence. It is a go-between between the company as client and the auditor as professional adviser. Its remit is to adopt an audit-specific perspective on:

(a) the company's internal controls;

(b) the company's relationship with the auditors; and

(c) the auditor's carrying out of the external control functions.

Review and monitoring

The audit sub-committee's focused remit is to keep under review the overall financial relationship between the company and the auditors. This will include:

(a) knowing the fee levels charged for the audit itself;

(b) knowing what other services the auditor provides. The Hampel Report talks of this situation – where the auditors also supply a 'substantial volume of non-audit services to the client' – providing a 'key role' for the audit sub-committee. Hampel recommends:

> We suggest that the committee should keep the nature and extent of such services under review, seeking to balance the maintenance of objectivity with value for money[6]

(c) monitoring the 10 per cent rule, i.e. does the company provide more than 10 per cent of the auditor's fee base? If it does, the relationship needs to be wound back below 10 per cent.

Watching out for fraud, etc.

Other roles falling to the audit committee include:

(a) business risk assessment and response;

(b) financial management;

(c) compliance with laws and regulations; and

(d) the safeguarding of assets, including minimising the risk of fraud.

Keeping in mind shareholder concerns

These criteria mean that shareholder concerns, i.e.

(a) getting value for the money spent by the board; and

(b) getting independent and unfettered financial expertise, etc;

remain the guiding principles in the relationship struck up between the board and the auditor.

Auditors and their external review function

The auditors have several specific external review functions in relation to the company's account and the outside world. These include:

(a) the accounts being 'true and fair': the auditors are required to answer the questions 'are the annual accounts properly prepared? Do they give a true and fair view?'

(b) 'going concern': the auditors are required to review the directors' statement on 'going concern';

(c) Cadbury Code compliance: the auditors will check for compliance by the company with certain elements of the Cadbury Code. These include the directors' report on the company's system of internal control;

(d) Greenbury compliance: the auditors are required to check aspects of the report of the board's remuneration committee; these include showing the breakdown between the various components of directors' remuneration packages.

Auditors getting it wrong: their legal position

The key UK case concerning auditors is *Caparo* v. *Dickman* (House of Lords 1990 2 AC 605).

Caparo involved auditors being sued for an audit which overvalued the worth of a company by a significant degree. The shareholders who sued the auditors had, in fact, launched a takeover bid on the basis of the accuracy of the audit.

The result was that the shareholders were not successful. The crucial question to be determined was: for what purpose was the audit prepared? The court decided, on the facts, that the audit had been prepared for the purpose of the shareholders generally and not for the narrower, more particular purpose of investment decisions being made by existing shareholders, i.e. such as launching a takeover bid by buying more shares in the company.

Caparo is still good law, but there is some confusion over the limits of the 'purposive' test (i.e. for what purpose is the audit prepared?). It is something of a moveable feast. As the Hampel Report notes, 'auditors feel inhibited in going beyond their present functions because of concerns about the present law on professional liability'.[6]

The *Caparo* case decision has been distinguished in *Morgan Crucible* v *Hill Samuel*.[7]

The facts of *Morgan Crucible* were as follows:

- there was a contested takeover bid;
- the directors and financial advisers made representations to the bidding company, knowing they would be relied on, i.e. the representations were made after the bidder had emerged;
- the matters discussed were financial assessments not as yet publicly available.

The purpose of the representations made in *Morgan Crucible* was deemed, on the facts, to be clear and specific, i.e. to an identified bidding company for the specific purpose of takeover deliberations. The auditors could not therefore rely on the general purpose proviso of *Caparo* to avoid liability.

How should auditors guard against liability for work they do?

Auditors need to be very clear about the task they are being required to perform and its particular parameters.

This involves assessing at each stage of the task:

(a) what is its purpose?

(b) who is its target audience?

(c) who will or seek to be able to rely on it?

From cases such as *Caparo* and *Morgan Crucible*, it can be said in general terms that:

- the later in the time process of the particular commercial transaction (i.e. takeover, sale, etc.) that the request for audit or financial verification, etc. is made of the auditor, then

- the more likely it is that a particular group will be able to rely on the accuracy of the auditor's work and seek legal redress if the auditor gets it wrong.

In summary, 'particular purpose' plus 'particular target audience' equates to particular 'caution' being deployed by the auditor.

What other problems are perceived in relation to auditors?

As we have already noted, the relationship between the company board and the auditors is supposed to be an independent relationship, i.e. the company acting through the board enlists the objective, arm's length assistance of the auditors.

However, in the late 1980s, in addition to carrying out their end-of-year audits, auditors sought to provide year-round advice. There were certainly perceptions that the ongoing board–auditor relationship made it more difficult for the auditors to sign off on the year-end accounts in an independent and objective capacity. These perceptions need to be closely guarded against.

Corporate governance issues to watch out for: auditors

Certain matters have been flagged by the Hampel Report as possibly undergoing change in the future. It is prudent therefore for the board and the company's auditors to keep a 'weather eye' on such issues and possible developments:

(a) the auditor's role regarding the half-yearly reports: as the Hampel Report notes, the scope of verification in addition to year-end results is 'evolving'.[8]

The report recommended the retention of the status quo, i.e. no verification of half-yearly results is required at this stage, which is referred to in terms of the present climate as 'verification for its own sake'.

(b) the board developing its own separate, internal audit function: the Cadbury Report saw it as good practice 'for companies to set up an internal function to help discharge the responsibilities of the audit committee' but did not go so far as to make it a Cadbury Code requirement.

In terms of a separate audit function, the Hampel Report:

- sees no need for a hard and fast rule; but
- believes that boards should review 'from time to time' the need for internal audit.[9]

> ## Auditors' template
>
> The following matters should be borne in mind by the board and auditors in terms of corporate governance strategy.
>
> - Are the auditors independent of the board and the company? This is fundamental to the audit process, as is the requirement that the auditors signing the accounts give a true and fair view (or a similar determination) in relation to the company's affairs.
>
> - Does work done by the auditor for the company supply the auditor with more than 10 per cent of its gross fees within a year? Both company and auditor should keep a close eye on this and try to keep it below 10 per cent.
>
> - Does the board have an audit sub-committee? An audit sub-committee can be a very effective vehicle for communication between the board and the auditors, and can allow for a streamlining of processes involved in compiling the audit.
>
> - Does the audit sub-committee comprise at least three non-executive directors, a majority of whom are independent of management?
>
> - What other work does the auditor do for the company? Work other than the audit may impinge on the auditor's independence.
>
> - Are the auditors fully aware of the board's corporate governance strategy? The auditors need to be kept abreast of any changes in company policy, and especially in terms of corporate governance methodology.

Notes

1. Hampel Report, page 49.
2. Willcock, J. (1998) Who's suing who? *The Independent*, 18 April.
3. Hampel Report, page 49.
4. Hampel Report, page 53.
5. Hampel Report, page 49.
6. Hampel Report page 52.
7. Hampel Report, pages 55–6.
8. 1991 Ch. 295.
9. Hampel Report, page 51.
10. Hampel Report, pages 54 and 64.

11

Financial issues: operating and financial review (OFR)

Background   113

OFR in the USA   113

The practical ramifications of OFR   114

Content of the OFR   115

Reviews   116

Particular risks to be identified in OFR   117

OFR template   117

Background

Operating and financial review (OFR) in its UK corporate governance context arises out of paragraph 4.53 of the Cadbury Report which stated that:

> the Committee recognises the advantage to users of reports and accounts of some explanation of the factors likely to influence their company's future progress. The inclusion of an essentially forward-looking Operating Only and Financial Review, along the lines developed by the Accounting Standards Board for consultation, would serve this purpose.

From this recommendation, OFR has taken on a life of its own.

In the UK, the OFR arose out of the Cadbury Report and work done by the Accounting Standards Board (the Accounting Standards Board issued a statement on the subject in July 1993).

In the ASB 1993 statement, OFR is defined as follows:

> A framework for the directors to discuss and analyse the business's performance and the factors underlying its result and financial position, in order to assist users to access for themselves the future potential of the business.

OFR in the USA

OFR as a UK development is somewhat behind the USA. In this respect, it is similar to several other corporate governance issues which have 'trickled across' the Atlantic. Other corporate governance issues in which the USA could be said to be taking a lead include:

(a) remuneration committees which have been established in the USA for some 20 years, but which have only really developed in the UK in the late 1980s and 1990s (see Chapter 6);

(b) the formal monitoring of board performance which has been led by the US National Association of Corporate Directors, who have recommended the introduction of formal procedures by which boards could access both their own collective performance and that of individual directors. The Hampel Report at paragraph 3.13 thought that, as far as the UK was concerned, it was too early to make any firm recommendations on the subject. They commented that some UK boards are already operating formal review procedures and that this was 'an interesting development' (see Chapter 4); and

(c) formal accounting guidelines to ensure consistency in the preparation and presentation of interim reports. Formal guidelines have formed part of the US and Canadian corporate landscape for some time, but are only now finding their way into the UK corporate environment (see Chapter 13).

In the USA, OFR is referred to as 'management discussion and analysis' (MD & A). MD & A is basically a filter designed to help shareholders and potential investors in a company to gain more clarity and insight in relation to the financial situation of the company. Its role is to present an analysis of the information found in a company's financial statement. To be of any use to investors, it must provide additional information on those matters contained in the financial statement (and simplify, when appropriate, for non-professional investors).

The practical ramifications of OFR

OFR is an emerging requirement of corporate governance. The practical ramifications of OFR, as with many other aspects of corporate governance, will continue to affect more and more companies. Some of the present practical ramifications of OFR are as follows.

Application to large listed companies

The Accounting Standards Board's OFR statement has been primarily aimed at listed companies. The rationale for this is that such companies are, by definition, operating with public funds and there is a legitimate public concern about how they operate.

Other large corporations

Other large corporations, which are not necessarily listed, but where there is a public interest in their financial performance and statements, should be adopting OFR.

Non-compulsion

Whilst OFR is not compulsory, the FTSE 100 companies have stepped into line and are producing OFR statements, although of varying quality.

'Trickle down'

The idea behind OFR is that it will be led by large companies and will trickle down to smaller companies as a matter of good practice. Smaller listed companies are urged by the Accounting Standards Board OFR statement to follow the spirit of the statement and to adapt it to suit their own circumstances.

Better shareholder communication

The main stream of OFR is seen as improving communication with shareholders and others.

Avoid adopting standard wording

The practice is developed in the USA where OFR's equivalent (the MD & A) makes for fairly poor reading because companies adopt dry language year on year, instead of tailoring the report to their specific, year-by-year position. This theme of 'anodyne reporting' we have seen also applies in other areas such as remuneration of directors. The whole spirit of the three corporate governance reports, especially the Hampel Report, constantly emphasises the need for corporate governance compliance to be tailor-made, i.e. to suit a particular company's needs, and not simply to regard corporate governance as a tiresome set of checklists to be ticked.

The OFR audience

It is not entirely clear to whom OFR is principally addressed. The target audience should not be defined too narrowly. It should take account of specialists, such as fund managers, accountants and other analysts. It should also, though, bear individual, private shareholders in mind.

Content of the OFR

There are four key requirements of the OFR statement.

The 'big picture'

This is described in the ASB statement as showing the 'top-down' structure of the business as a whole. This part of the OFR is attempting to contextualise the company's business in terms of the wider market place and community. Once this is mapped out, the OFR can delve into the sub-issues flowing from the big picture.

Objective discussion

The OFR has the difficult task of being an objective analysis of the company's financial position. As such, both good news events and bad news events need to be given equal treatment in neutral language.

Explaining the main features of the business

This requires the OFR to set out the 'shocks', 'bumps', good news events, etc. that have affected, or are likely to affect, the business. There needs to be something more than the simple provision of numbers; there needs to be explanation that underpins the figures. This requires a breakdown of the various components of the business and their impact on the overall results. It is about linking and explaining various parts of the business. It is also about explaining and interpreting particular risks to specific parts of the business.

Reviews

As part of the OFR, there are two reviews: the operating review and the financial review.

The operating review deals with the four key items as follows:

- current-year issues which will impact on future-year prospects;
- issues which may affect the business (this will involve some guesswork, so it needs to be factored at a fairly conservative level);
- the interpretation of financial ratios relevant to the company; and
- investment plans of the company for future use.

The financial review is supposed to follow a checklist provided as part of the Accounting Standards Board statement. Amongst the issues on the ASB checklist are the following:

- treasury policy;
- borrowing policy, gearing and interest repayment;
- factoring in events and possible events which may affect the business;
- ongoing issues, which may affect future years;
- tax liabilities;
- cash flow;
- liquidity at the end of financial year, together with a chart of borrowing over the course of the 12-month financial period.

Several of these items have been regarded as sensitive, and companies have not given much away in terms of their OFRs.

Particular risks to be identified in OFR

The sorts of matters that the OFR should pick up in terms of problems, risks or shocks the company has, or may face, include the following:

- employee shortages (for example, the lack of a certain skills base as and when required);
- similarly, shortage of raw materials;
- intellectual property issues such as patency trademarks, etc;
- litigation liabilities;
- environmental liabilities;
- insurance;
- health and safety issues;
- product liability concerns;
- overdependence on a major supplier or customer;
- exchange rate fluctuations where a company's business is exposed to particularly volatile markets;
- inflation divergence between certain markets.

OFR template

The following represents some key corporate governance issues regarding OFR.

- OFR is not yet compulsory but is certainly seen as necessary by FTSE 100 companies.
- OFR will trickle down to smaller companies.
- OFR statements should avoid using year-on-year repeat formula wording, and should be tailored to a particular company's requirements.
- The anticipated audience of the OFR should include both the specialist and the non-specialist.

- There is no 'set length' for an OFR, but if it is to operate effectively within the spirit of the ASB 1993 statement, the emerging practice suggests that an OFR of between four and six pages will need to be prepared.

- The OFR needs to go 'behind the numbers', and the figures need to provide explanation on the basis of the 'big picture' of the company.

- Particular shocks or events affecting the company (or forthcoming or anticipated such issues) should be highlighted and explained in terms of the company's performance.

- The public relations ramifications of OFR seem to be similar to other areas of corporate governance, i.e. open and honest communication is generally the best policy so that potential 'bad news' can be managed more effectively. There is recognition, though, that too much 'gloom and doom' could unnecessarily affect the company's share price.

- OFR is likely to increase due to market pressure, peer-competitor pressure and the wider corporate environment.

12

Financial issues: going concern

Background 121

The going concern statement 122

The content of going concern statements 123

Going concern template 123

Background

The 'going concern' issue has formed part of the corporate governance project in the UK since the Cadbury Report of 1992. At paragraph 4.6, the Cadbury Code of Best Practice provides as follows:

> the director should report that the business is a going concern, with supporting assumptions or qualifications as necessary.

As fiduciaries to the company, directors owe standards of both trust and competence. In financial terms, the ramifications of the directors falling short of these standards is principally set out in the Insolvency Act 1986. Section 214 of the Insolvency Act 1986 deals with 'wrongful trading', which is a situation where a company is accruing losses or is in poor financial shape, and the directors fail to take sufficient steps to ascertain the exact situation and to remedy it. A charge of wrongful trading can give rise to personal liability on the part of the directors, i.e. they could be called upon to contribute from their personal assets to the debts of the company. Wrongful trading plans will arrive in the context of the liquidation of the company, and it will be the liquidator who will pursue such actions.

Against this background, the going concern requirement of the directors in the financial statements is of critical importance. The directors need to be sure of the grounds upon which they claim the company is a going concern. Obviously, the conclusion that the company is a going concern will be made after the work of the following groups has been completed:

- The board of directors;
- Any audit sub-committee reporting to the board of directors;
- Any internal audit function;
- The external auditors and any other relevant groups.

The going concern requirement may appear to many companies to be unproblematic, i.e. they have traded successfully for long periods and have never had any financial problems to note. However, this assumption, based on the history of the company, ignores the more volatile environment of the 1990s and the fact that statistical evidence would suggest that more than one in five quoted non-financial companies 'is at risk of either insolvency or of a major reconstruction to avoid insolvency within the next three years' (this information has been assembled by the company Syspas Limited).

The going concern statement

The London Stock Exchange Listing Rules provide that, for all accounting periods after 31 December 1995, the directors must report that the business is a going concern and must also provide supporting assumptions or qualifications.

As well as Stock Exchange Listing Rules, there is a system of 'guidance', which has been developed by the accounting profession and finance directors and is set out in a document entitled 'going concern and financial reporting'. This document provides that the going concern status of the company should be set out as part of the OFR of the company. This guidance document provides that the directors should come to one of three conclusions.

Going concern without qualification

The company will continue to operate as a going concern for the foreseeable future, and the going concern basis is appropriate in preparing accounts.

Going concern but subject to doubts

The company should be able to continue as a going concern, but there is some doubt about it. However, that doubt is not sufficient to not claim a going concern basis in terms of preparing a set of financial accounts.

Not a going concern

The company will not be able to continue to operate as a going concern and therefore the directors cannot claim that as the basis on which to draw up the financial statement.

It is particularly important that factors which may cast doubt on the going concern requirement are identified and explained. Such factors may include the following matters:

- the amount and status of borrowings;
- the type of such borrowings, for instance whether they are on-demand borrowings which could be called up at any time;
- the state of play with the company's auditors;
- the economic climate.

The content of going concern statements

The going concern statements are usually about a paragraph in length and state:

- that enquiries, due consideration, review, etc. have been conducted by the directors;
- that the directors have formed a judgement, a view, a considered opinion, etc.;
- that such judgement has been formed at the time of approving the financial statements;
- and, on the basis of the foregoing points, that the directors continue to adopt the going concern basis in preparing the financial statements.

Other matters which may be factored into the going concern statement include reference to the economic conditions in which the company has been operating in respect of:

- customers;
- the type of business it is;
- trading prospects;
- capital requirements;
- borrowings, etc.;
- 'adequate resources';
- projected gearing ratios;
- liquid resources;
- expenditure plans;
- cash requirements.

Going concern template

The following matters should be borne in mind in terms of the going concern requirement.

- The going concern statement can only be made in the light of the financial and accounting systems of the company being efficient and working under the aegis of the board. This means bringing together the work of the audit sub-committee, the auditors, the internal audit, and so on.

- Care should be taken to identify risks whether they exist or are on the horizon.
- Consideration of the going concern statement should take place as early as possible, i.e. not left to year-end, so that potential or current problems can be factored in and dealt with at an early opportunity.
- There needs to be sufficient forward momentum in financial statements for the auditors to work with the current period and also make projections about the following financial period.
- There should be a board paper prepared on going concern issues so that the board is apprised of any current issues, and can therefore speak with one voice and plan remedial action on a united basis.

13

Financial issues: interim reporting

Background 127

Stock Exchange requirements as to interim reporting 127

Current issues 128

The Cadbury Report and interim reporting 128

Compulsory interim reporting standards 129

Interim reporting template 130

Background

The Cadbury Report at paragraph 1.2 specifically provided that 'financial reporting and accountability' were part of its enquiries.

The three broad areas of enquiry noted by Cadbury were:

- the control and reporting functions of the board of directors;
- the role of the auditors;
- financial reporting and accountability.

Cadbury went on to confirm that its proposals were to 'contribute positively to the promotion of good corporate governance as a whole'. Financial reporting, including interim financial reporting, has therefore been an integral part of the corporate governance project in the UK in the 1990s.

Unlike other areas of corporate governance, the interim reporting requirement has been around for some three decades. Interim reporting has been compulsory for companies listed on the London Stock Exchange since 1964. Such requirements are set out in the Stock Exchange Yellow Book.

Stock Exchange requirements as to interim reporting

The Yellow Book requires an interim financial report on profit and loss which includes reference to the following matters:

- profit or loss before taxation;
- extraordinary items forming part of the profit and loss;
- nett turnover;
- shareholder matters such as profit or loss attributable to shareholders;
- the rate of dividends paid to shareholders;
- earnings per share;
- significant information allowing investors to make an informed assessment of the overall trends of the group's activities and its profit and loss position;
- the explanation of any special factors affecting profit and loss for the period;
- comparisons with corresponding periods in the previous year;
- comments on the company's prospects for the rest of the financial year.

Timing of interim reports

The interim report has to be published within four months of the end of the company's half year to which it relates.

Interim reporting under the Listing Rules

As with many items of corporate governance, companies have taken varying stances in relation to the interim reporting requirements. These range on a spectrum from:

- 'Best practice', which adopts the letter and spirit of the Yellow Book requirements and which involves companies essentially publishing mini-versions of their end-of-year annual reports.
- *De minimus* approaches which involve the company complying with the bare necessities as required by the Yellow Book.

Current issues

Among the current issues concerning interim reporting are the following.

- The UK does not have comprehensive accounting guidelines in relation to interim reporting which would help to provide consistency in their preparation of presentation (this is unlike the USA and Canada).
- However, the London Stock Exchange is focusing on key issues such as insider dealing. Since 1992 it has published a document known as *Guidance on the Dissemination of Price Sensitive Information*. The document aims to ensure that information is fairly available in the public domain, rather than disclosed to particular people or selectively to groups who can then take advantage of it.

The Cadbury Report and interim reporting

Cadbury focused on interim reporting, as we have seen above, and made the following recommendations:

Balance sheet information

Cadbury recommended that balance sheet information should be included as part of the interim report and should be reviewed by the auditors.

Yellow Book requirements

The requirements of the London Stock Exchange should be monitored and reviewed and should provide that balance sheet information be part of the interim report.

Clarification of accounting standards

Cadbury recommended that the accounting standards should be standardised, i.e. as is the case in the USA and Canada for the preparation of interim reports.

Cash flow information

Cash flow information should be considered by committees after Cadbury.

As a result of these board recommendations, the Accounting Standards Board, in December 1996, produced a draft on interim reports. The Accounting Standards Board draft statement will be an example of best practice rather than compulsory.

Compulsory interim reporting standards

Whereas the Accounting Standards Board has provided good practice standards, the International Accounting Standards Committee (IASC) has begun work on developing an 'International Accounting Standard' which provides information that companies must follow in preparing their interim reports. The draft IASC statement is detailed, and any final standard is likely to be the same.

The draft IASC statement of principles on interim financial reporting includes reference to the following matters.

- The standard will be compulsory, i.e. companies will not be able to contract out of it, or vary it according to their circumstances.
- The minimum requirements of an interim report should include: summaries of the balance sheet, profit and loss account and cash flow statement, together with explanatory notes.
- As far as the balance sheet is concerned, it should include reference to the latest year-end balance sheet (at least the key figures from that document).
- Likewise with the previous profit and loss account, its key figures should be included in the interim profit and loss account.
- As to the cash flow, it should be broken down into operating, investing and financing activities and should provide a reconciliation of cash movements within the period.

- The notes should include reference to exceptional items, breakdown of different parts of the business, comments on particular time-of-year issues (e.g. quiet trading periods) and significant post balance sheet events.

Interim reporting template

- The present minimum requirements are set out in the Yellow Book for listed companies. Listed companies need to comply with those requirements to retain their listings.

- The Accounting Standards Board has published good practice guidelines for interim accounting.

- The International Accounting Standards Committee (IASC) will be introducing a compulsory statement of principles, which companies must follow. This will apply to listed companies working internationally.

- The two available approaches – the discrete approach in which each interim report is regarded on a stand-alone basis and the integral approach, i.e. where the interim report is incorporated as part of the end-of-year report – are available. Each has their particular advantages and disadvantages. For example, a disadvantage with the discrete approach is that a company suffering from marked seasonal differences will have an interim report which differs widely from its end-of-year report.

- The costs of interim reporting will necessarily increase as standards rise.

- Some companies are contemplating quarterly interim reporting; this would seem to be an example of where the Hampel Report claims that too much emphasis is going into governance at the expense of profit making, i.e. involves companies looking over their shoulder and not concentrating on the bottom line.

- Interim reports should be precise and to the point, i.e. they do not need the detail of an end-of-year report.

- As with other areas of corporate governance, companies need to produce an interim report which meets their own needs.

- The board, together with internal and external auditors and others, should be working in a timely and efficient manner on producing the interim report; this will require providing sufficient resources to meet a company's needs.

- Advertising the interim report rather than sending it to each individual shareholder may prove cost-effective.

14

Corporate governance for the shareholders

An overview   133

The shareholder's legal position generally   133

The importance of 'shareholder returns'   135

The role of the shareholders in the corporate governance matrix   135

The role of institutional shareholders in corporate governance   138

Shareholders' template   142

An overview

Shareholding; 'spread' and 'depth'

There are now something like 13 million individuals in the UK who own shares. This shareholding revolution follows in the footsteps of government industry privatisations begun in the 1980s (see Chapters 2 and 17). The 'breadth' of shareholding is more than matched, however, by its 'depth'. By depth, we mean the concentration of share ownership in institutional hands. The Hampel Report estimates that '60% of shares in listed UK companies are held by UK institutions – pension funds, insurance companies, unit and investment trusts. Of the remaining 40%, about half are owned by individuals and half by overseas owners, mainly institutions.'[1]

Shareholders and PR

In terms of corporate governance issues, most of the focus of attention is on the institutional shareholders, but we shouldn't underestimate the growing importance of individual shareholders (especially when they band together). Their ability to attract publicity by, for example, the display of a farmyard pig in its own swill outside an AGM to show their displeasure at, say, levels of boardroom pay can be quite devastating. The board locked inside the AGM venue is virtually helpless to control the media field day which ensues. As we noted in Chapter 2 (and will mention again in Chapter 17), public relations (PR) is set to be a key battleground of ongoing corporate governance developments. Media treatments and perceptions of company business will assume increasingly greater importance in a society ever more reliant on 'spin-doctored' and 'spin-countered' electronic images.

The shareholder's legal position generally

Rights

The shareholders usually have a set of general rights, subject to the specific position adopted as part of their 'contract' with the company, comprising:

(a) the general documents – the articles of association and any shareholder's agreement; and

(b) the specific document – the contract of allotment concerning the shares themselves.

The usual rights include:

(a) a right to receive notices of general meetings including the AGM;

(b) a right to attend general meetings;

(c) a right to vote; and

(d) a right to a dividend (where one has been declared by the directors).

Shareholders also have the right not to be 'treated unfairly': that is, for example, to have their shareholding suffer unnecessarily in terms of diminution in value. Under section 459 of the Companies Act 1985, the shareholder who has been treated unfairly by the board can petition the court and, if the court is satisfied of the shareholder's allegations, the court has wide powers, including ordering the company to purchase the disgruntled shareholder's shares.

There are also, currently, proposals to increase the ability of shareholders to seek redress from directors they allege to have managed and controlled the company in a negligent (i.e. careless) manner.

Duties

Generally

Generally shareholders can act in their own self-interests; this translates into their voting at shareholders' meetings however they wish. Putting themselves first is no barrier.

There are, however, two types of shareholder requiring special consideration.

Majority shareholders

This general rule as to shareholders voting as they wish 'cuts out', however, for 'majority' shareholders, i.e. for those holding a majority of shares on their own or voting with others and making up a majority block. *Clemens*' case[2] provides that, before voting, majority shareholders must have regard to 'equitable considerations'.

This is somewhat vague; essentially, it means that such shareholders should be motivated by commercial reasons and should be able to justify their vote on the basis of it being broadly in the company's best interests.

Institutional shareholders

See below, page 138.

The importance of 'shareholder returns'

The shareholders are the central target of corporate governance compliance. It is chiefly for them that the corporate governance matrix has been put in place. It is not exclusively for them (as the wider definition of the stakeholder concept set out in Chapter 2 indicates), but they are the linchpin of it, the central focus, certainly, of the Hampel Committee's findings.

The focus of UK companies: shareholder returns

> The single overriding objective shared by all listed companies, whatever their size or type of business, is the preservation and the greatest practicable enhancement over time of their shareholders' investment. All boards have this responsibility and their policies, structure, composition and governing processes should reflect this.[3]

This contrasts with the Japanese model of company philosophy which places employees ahead of shareholders (see Chapter 15).

US companies: also 'narrow focus'

This squares with Michael Novak's idea that American companies are narrow focus organisations. Companies are built, Novak claims:

> to attain quite particular purposes, often purposes that tend to come around again quite continuously, as restaurants are built to feed people day after day. Enterprise associations are focused, purposive, instrumental, and executive: they fix a purpose and execute it.[4]

As Novak also notes of the USA, publicly owned companies account for 1 per cent of all business organisations but 'produce more than half of America's economic output'.[5]

The role of the shareholders in the corporate governance matrix

The shareholders have several diverse overseeing and monitoring roles in terms of corporate governance. The main thrust of corporate governance is to provide fairness and clarity for shareholders which, in turn, underlines the guiding principle of UK companies – to maximise shareholder returns within the given parameters. The Hampel Report refers to this concept under the umbrella term 'shareholder value'.[6]

As was pointed out in the overview in Chapter 6, a distinction can be drawn between the role played by:

- individual shareholders; and
- institutional shareholders.

General corporate governance inputs

Among the general corporate governance roles played by shareholders are the following.

PR strategies

Examples are boardroom excess; perceptions of fairness; directors' pay is a live issue. It was not simply put away by the three reports. A vigilant approach is required.

Monitoring: annual reporting

The annual return and the audit process are aimed at providing the shareholders with a full, balanced and accurate picture of the company's performance.

The annual general meeting (AGM)

The AGM represents the board's 'judgement day', when the roles of the auditors, the shareholders and other stakeholders come together to judge:

- the collective performance of the board;
- the individual performance of various directors (for example, the work of the CEO); and
- the work of the board's various sub-committees: appointment, remuneration and audit.

General aims of the AGM

To allow small shareholders to:

(a) be fully briefed on company activities;

(b) question senior management on both operations and governance.

Notice to shareholders

For AGMs, at least 20 working days' notice (i.e. reference to working days excludes weekends) should be given to shareholders (Hampel Report, page 47). This is in excess of the Companies Act 1985, which requires 21 days' clear notice (which includes weekends as well as weekdays).

Resumés of proposed business to be circulated?

Boards should consider this if it is helpful in making proposals more accessible to shareholders.

Questioning of the board

This is to be encouraged especially when senior management is available to field questions on policy, etc.

Questioning of the chairman of the audit committee

The chairman should be available to be questioned on audit-related matters at the AGM.[7]

AGM overhaul issues to consider

There are two Hampel Report recommendations designed to make the AGM more 'meaningful and interesting'. They are:

(a) the inclusion of question and answer sessions; and

(b) the announcement of the number of proxy votes.[8]

Postal voting

Postal voting should be avoided because it might be perceived as stifling the chance for face-to-face debate at the AGM.[9]

Providing written answers

The Hampel Report recommends that the chairman should 'undertake to provide the questioner with a written answer to any significant question which cannot be answered on the spot'.[10]

The role of institutional shareholders in corporate governance

Background

As was noted at the outset of this chapter, the role of institutional shareholders is crucial in the running of public companies. Many institutional shareholders will have dedicated corporate governance departments. Their central role will be to attend and vote at meetings in which they control large parcels of shares on behalf of their clients. Such parcels of shares will often be critical to management of the company. A parcel of shares may give a controlling interest in the company to one faction over another.

In broad terms, a company can be controlled when shareholders whose shares account for 50 per cent or more of the issued share capital get together. An ordinary resolution at a shareholders' meeting will require 50 per cent plus one of the votes. A special resolution, on the other hand, will require 75 per cent of the votes cast. Special resolution status effectively means that total control is given to one group or another. There may, therefore, be a premium price payable in respect of shares which trigger a change in either the 50 per cent or 75 per cent thresholds. This will obviously mean attending the meetings and vetting the resolutions to be submitted to such meetings. The bottom line for institutional shareholders will be to protect the value of investments which they hold on behalf of their own stakeholders – pension funds, insurance funds, etc.

The role of the institutional shareholders within the company

The general multiple role of the institutional shareholders is:

- to participate in and vote at shareholder meetings (only 40 per cent of shares are currently voted on, according to the Hampel Report);[11]
- to be responsible to their clients for making considered use of their vote;[12]
- to consider the board's proposals;
- to bring objective judgement and the expertise of another 'professional perspective' to bear on the company.

Financial decision making

As far as takeover bids and other key company occurrences are concerned, institutional shareholders do not so much as vote with their feet (by attending the AGM as has traditionally been the case) as over the telephone and by other less formal methods. As controllers of large parcels of shares within the company, it is inevitable that institutional shareholders wield a considerable degree of control, which filters through to the board at both formal and informal levels.

For instance, it will be made known to the board whether a chief executive officer or managing director meets with institutional shareholder approval. The communication channels open to the institutional shareholders to get their message across are more varied and more subtle than those available to an individual shareholder.

As with political parties who seek the crucial support of swinging voters, and devote a great deal of time, energy and resources to 'winning them over', so too is the case with the competing corporate parties, as far as the key institutional shareholders are concerned, in terms of events such as hostile company takeovers.

A good example of the 'kingmaker' role played by an institutional shareholder was provided during the long and hostile takeover of the Forte Crest hotel group by Granada. At the end of the day, the linchpin of Granada's success was the support for its bid by Mercury Asset Management, the major institutional shareholder in Forte.

To facilitate better communication

The board and the institutional directors should have an open and regular dialogue and hold meetings with pre-agreed agendas. Care should be taken by the board, however, to avoid giving away price-sensitive information, or in any way 'favouring' the institutional shareholders ahead of other shareholders and other groups.

It is inevitable, however, given the powerful position which institutional shareholders find themselves in, in relation to the day-to-day management and governance of the companies, that their positions in the power structures are quite different from, and superior to, those of individual shareholders.

What we are really talking about is an élite group of professional shareholders whose livelihoods depend on the quality of their investment decision making, rather than individuals who hold shares as part of a portfolio of personal assets. For the institutional shareholder, the quality of the investment decisions will ultimately reflect on their job status, promotion prospects, etc. They will therefore be, or should be, objective when it comes to bringing about changes in a company when those changes are considered necessary.

Institutional shareholders within the corporate governance matrix

Institutional shareholders have an important part to play in implementing the work done by the Cadbury, Greenbury and Hampel Reports.

Institutional shareholders have their own set of stakeholders – including those with pension funds invested, insurance policies, etc. Institutional shareholders effectively have two tiers of customers: the corporations and other employers who invest funds, and secondly, the employees and other individuals whose funds are marshalled through their employers.

Some of the matters which are essential to institutional shareholder concerns within corporate governance are as follows.

- Institutional shareholders need an open and honest relationship with management, and ideally should be in a long-term relationship with a particular company.
- Where there is a loss of confidence in the company or management, for whatever reason, there needs to be an acknowledgement by all concerned that remedial action needs to be taken.
- In the light of the ongoing relationship between the institutional shareholder and the company, and the fact that the institutional shareholder is likely to be the largest shareholder, institutional shareholders are ideally placed to monitor events and to map out strategies in conjunction with the company.
- Institutional directors can play a crucial role in particularly sensitive issues, such as the levels of directors' remuneration.

Corporate governance issues for institutional shareholders

Among the corporate governance issues to which institutional shareholders will pay particular attention, are the following.

- The role of chairman and chief executive of the company should not be combined because of the concentration of power this can lead to within the company, e.g. the Robert Maxwell scenario.
- The role of non-executive directors on the board as providing rigorous, independent viewpoints is crucial.

- As well as being independent, non-executive directors should receive appropriate training.
- The appointment of directors should be a transparent and objective process, and directors should be put up for re-appointment at least every three years.
- The audit committee should be made up, ideally, solely of non-executive directors.
- The non-executive directors should have clear lines of communication available to the company's external auditors.
- The directors' remuneration committees should be composed solely of independent non-executive directors.
- There is a recognition that, for smaller companies, the above requirements will need to be relaxed to meet particular circumstances, i.e. it may be impractical or not cost-effective to follow each of the criteria. In summary, smaller companies need to adopt those of the above criteria which they can realistically meet. However, the goal for each company should be full compliance with the above list.

The mechanics of institutional shareholder involvement

There is no code as to how institutional shareholders will, or should, operate in relation to the companies in which they control major parcels of shares. Practice has therefore evolved in an *ad hoc* and piecemeal fashion.

The mechanics of institutional shareholder involvement will include the following.

- There should be perusal of all company resolutions going before extraordinary general meetings and annual general meetings.
- There will be dialogue between the corporate governance department of the institutional shareholder and the department which actively manages the funds.
- Negotiations with particular companies take place privately rather than in the glare of the shareholders' meeting. This means, essentially, that the views and influence of the institutional shareholders have been known and factored into any decision making, ahead of the meeting itself.
- The institutional shareholders are in constant consultation with other institutions and with the company board.
- Face-to-face meetings with company management are particularly important for institutional shareholders. They can make known particular objections and criteria for management, e.g. in relation to remuneration.
- There should be liaison with the company's advisers, stockbrokers and others.

Trends in institutional shareholding and corporate governance

The trend is that institutional shareholders are likely to become more important in terms of corporate governance compliance.

Institutional shareholders have been criticised for favouring management ahead of shareholders – this can be characterised as supporting the status quo against reform.

There is a growing acknowledgement within institutional shareholding factions that the dialogue between a company and its institutional shareholders will need to become more transparent over time. This is because the role of the individual shareholder is becoming more crucial (in the light of public relations issues, etc.) and the fact that individual shareholders now have access to much better means of communication and are able to keep up to date with company matters more efficiently.

Shareholders' template

- The board's first objective in general, and in relation to corporate governance policy in particular, is to maximise shareholder returns.
- The board should not 'bundle' issues under the umbrella of one resolution but keep them as separate resolutions with separate votes taken.[13]
- The board should be careful not to favour institutional shareholders with price-sensitive information, etc.[14]
- Good communication is vital between a company and its shareholders; it remains a tenet of developing corporate governance – see the case studies.
- The board should maintain regular and efficient means of communication with both institutional shareholders and individual shareholders.
- The board should try to seek the views of shareholders in relation to corporate governance compliance by the company.
- The board should bear in mind the opinions of shareholders in relation to contentious, or potentially contentious, proposals.
- Directors' remuneration should be particularly well handled in terms of communications with shareholders.
- The appointment process for directors should be carefully considered, and should be transparent, and in all cases proceed on the basis of selecting the best candidate available to meet the company's objective criteria.

- Institutional shareholders, in particular, are crucial to a company's profit performance and to its corporate governance strategies and compliance. They should be seen as partners in corporate governance issues.
- The board should, as elsewhere, bear in mind considerations on the basis of the company's specific set-up and avoid the box-ticking approach to corporate governance.

Notes

1. Hampel Report, page 40.
2. 1976 2 All ER 268.
3. Hampel Report, page 11.
4. Michael Novak, page 5.
5. Michael Novak, page 4.
6. Hampel Report, page 8.
7. Hampel Report, page 46.
8. Hampel Report, page 45.
9. Hampel Report, page 45.
10. Hampel Report, page 46.
11. Hampel Report, page 41.
12. Hampel Report, page 41.
13. Hampel Report, page 46.
14. Hampel Report, page 44.

15

Corporate governance for the company's employees

The employee's role in the company   147

The employee's legal position   147

The role of the employees in the UK corporate governance matrix   148

The Asian corporate model: employees first   149

Employee template   150

The employee's role in the company

The employees are a key part of the business. Their commitment and loyalty will generate goodwill and translate into profits.

The employee's legal position

Service agreements

The employees are contractually bound by the terms of their service agreements.

In return for their emoluments package, they will be bound by the usual employee commitments, including the following.

Confidentiality

Keeping the company's secrets both during their time with the company and after they leave.

Commitment to the company

Devoting their time and attention to the company's business.

Non-competition

- Not competing with the business during their period of employment with the company and complying with reasonable restraint of trade clauses once they leave the employer.

- Restraint of trade clauses must be reasonable to be upheld by the court. They will usually be found in the service agreement, and they will seek to limit the type of work and the location of work of an employee once the employee has left the employer.

- The elements of a restraint of trade clause are time, usually expressed in years, and distance (normally expressed as being within a radius of the place of business of the employer).

- Legal principles developed over the years have concluded that a restraint of trade is void, i.e. of no legal effect, if it is not reasonable in its term. Therefore, restraints of trade will often be drafted allowing for a series of options, e.g. three years, two years, one year, and so on, and 50 miles, 25 miles, 10 miles, etc., so that they can be adjusted to meet the particular circumstances of an employee.

- The more senior an employee, the more likely it is that such an employee will have shared in trades and other secrets and a court is more likely to uphold a fairly onerous restraint of trade clause. The employee, on the other hand, will argue that an onerous restraint is an undue restriction on ability to earn a living.

The board's relationship to the employees

The board of directors has to bear in mind the interests of the employees (section 309, Companies Act 1985).

In terms of general law and corporate governance, the shareholders' interests come before those of the employees, but as section 309 reflects, the employees do have an important role to play in UK corporate governance.

The role of the employees in the UK corporate governance matrix

The employees are an important focus of corporate governance policy. One manifestation of this is the phenomenon of 'cascade briefing'.[1]

Cascade briefing

'Cascade briefing' refers to the flow, through a company, of information emanating from the board, where top management briefs middle management who, in turn, brief junior management, and so on, down through the employee ranks. As an ideal, cascade briefing is worth pursuing, subject to ensuring that a company's confidentiality requirements, etc. are met.

Communicating with employees

Care needs to be taken as to the type of information which is relayed to employees and the manner of that relay. The method will depend on an industry-by-industry set of criteria. For example, in the car industry, it may be efficient to do it by in-house video at the workplace rather than by giving employees 'homework' to take home to read.

There are various methods of getting messages across, including noticeboards, line managers, meetings, in-house publications, in-house videos, etc.

It will be important for the board that it controls, and is seen to control, the sort of information that makes its way to employees. Given the old adage that bad news travels fast, it is important that the board accurately and honestly communicates with employees and does not leave them in an uncertain position, where the worst case scenario becomes part of their thinking.

The Asian corporate model: employees first

Whereas UK and US companies are narrow-focus, shareholder-first enterprises, Japanese companies put much more emphasis on the interests of employees (i.e. providing employment whenever it can) and a broader 'community-based' ethos. Shareholder concerns do not rank nearly as highly as they do in the UK.

A clear example of this differing philosophy is provided by the following extract from Kentaro Aikawa, Chairman of Mitsubishi Heavy Industries. As the extract indicates, the mind-set of the board in Asian countries is vastly different to that of the UK model. Mr Aikawa recently declared:

> After careful consideration, the board has decided that in future the company will put more emphasis on employment than profit. Our profit margin is going to be 6% – no higher, no lower. If it looks like we will make more money than expected, then we will take on more orders at lower prices in order to adjust the figure. We are a manufacturing company and the main purpose of what we do is to use facilities and labour in a stable manner and at maximum capacity.
>
> If we make too much money on what we produce, it drives up the price of other products, which is bad for everyone. The social effects of what we do must be our primary consideration. We will not, I repeat not, give our shareholders precedence. I know that if we were an American company we would come under intense criticism for saying these things, and they would get me into trouble with my finance department. But we do not need to advertise to foreigners to get them to buy our stock. If our stock has no appeal for investors, they can sell it straight away. Our employees have no such freedom of choice, and it is primarily for them that we exist.[2]

As Jeremy Warner writes, this statement would be 'shocking' were it delivered by a City or Wall Street chairman because it insists that 'the primary purpose of business is not that of serving shareholders; it is the wider interests of company, community and nation that come first'.[2]

> **Employee template**
>
> Among the corporate governance strategies which should be adopted in relation to employers are the following.
>
> - Tailor-made communication strategies with the employees as a whole, and with particular groups of employees, should be adopted by the board to meet their own particular circumstances.
> - Different methods of communication should be experimented with so as to ascertain the premium means of communication.
> - The interests of employees are part of the statutory responsibility of the board.
> - It should be borne in mind that employees will focus on rumour and innuendo and put a negative spin on matters, unless communication channels are open and are unambiguous and controlled by the board.
> - Management should be skilled in communicating with the employees.
> - Methods such as 'cascade briefing' should be continually refined to ensure efficient and clear communication channels are maintained.
> - Employees are an absolutely vital link in the corporate governance chains. Boardrooms need to consider, of course, that it is not only employees, but their families, friends and other associates, who will inevitably get to hear about poor communication which emanates from the board.

Notes

1 *The Corporate Governance Handbook*, Chapter 9.

2 Warner, J. (1998) Stakeholding gone mad, or is this the future?, *The Independent*, 18 April, p. 21.

16

Corporate governance and the company's regulators

Identifying a company's regulators   153

Formal regulation   153

Informal regulation   154

Environmental concerns   155

The corporate governance matrix   157

The emerging corporate governance matrix in tabular form   157

Identifying a company's regulators

A company is regulated by several external parties, whose task is to keep the company operating with regard to certain statutory and other boundaries. Such groups are 'interested parties' in the company on a broad basis. Their roles can be divided into a formal, official basis and an informal, unofficial basis.

Formal regulation

Among the formal regulators of companies in the UK are the following entities.

The taxation authorities

These are for both corporation tax on assessable profits earned by the company and on wages earned by employees and directors' fees paid to management. This regulatory mode takes place on an annual basis, subject to greater scrutiny from time to time. In addition, there is VAT registration for companies with an annual turnover of more than £50 000.

Companies House

The companies registrar is based in Cardiff and is charged with maintaining company public records in accordance with the Companies Act 1985 as amended. Amongst other documents, the annual returns for a company must be lodged at Companies House.

The Stock Exchange

The Stock Exchange regulates the public sale of shares and securities. It requires listed companies to include corporate governance statements in their annual returns, etc.

Audit and accounting bodies

These are the professional bodies to which company auditors belong and which set and monitor reporting standards.

Administrative receivers

These are typically appointed by banks and other secured creditors and their role is to go into the company, replace the board, run the company as a going concern and recoup the money owed to the appointing creditor. Whilst in theory it is a going concern remedy, what often happens is that the resultant bad publicity, loss of customer and investor confidence, and sale of the best assets means that the company inevitably slips into liquidation (i.e. a 'winding-up' procedure as opposed to a going concern procedure).

Liquidation

The liquidation process involves the liquidator:

(a) seizing the company assets; and

(b) distributing them either in cash or kind (i.e. non-cash) to creditors and others according to a statutory order or list (set out in the Insolvency Act 1986).

The process ends with the company being struck off the register of companies, so that it no longer exists.

Informal regulation

This includes a range of interested parties and phenomena affecting a company:

Customers

This will include new customers, potential customers, existing customers, key customers. The company's performance in relation to its customers is becoming ever more critical as marketing and public relations departments boom within certain sectors.

Competitors

A natural benchmark for a company will be the performance of its competitors across a range of criteria. The company and its board should be continually assessing where in the spectrum the company lies, in terms of its quality and performance in relation to its competitors, and be seeking to attain a better market share and a better share price as a result of improvement. A good example in the public sector, in recent years, of companies performing rigorously against each other and innovating on that basis is provided by the supermarket chains.

Lobby groups

(a) Consumer groups: as customers and others become more organised through better technology and communications, the focus on customer and consumer awareness is raised in any event and is increased by organised consumer groups.

(b) Environmental groups: this is discussed below.

Media scrutiny

Companies have the potential to provide a rich seam of stories which attract media attention. This is particularly the case with directors' remuneration, directors who speak off the record about company performance, shareholder disillusion and other such matters.

Environmental concerns

Environmental concerns have been on the agenda for companies since the 1960s and 1970s and were exacerbated in the early 1970s by the oil crisis in the Middle East. Since then, of course, there has been regular high drama associated with the environmental stories: oil spills involving supertankers; fires in rainforests; clearing of forests around the world; the nuclear meltdown in Chernobyl; motor vehicle pollution and numbers and the concept of 'gridlock' in cities around the world; the dumping of industrial waste, including particular issues such as the Brent Spa oil rig.

Developing environmental risk management

Underlying a company's wish to develop an environmental risk management approach are two influences:

- minimising bad publicity in which the company could be characterised as reckless towards the environment; and
- obtaining competitive advantage by fostering the company's environmentally responsible image.

To date, there are no agreed environmental standards which need to be met by a company. The starting point is British Standard BS 7750, which can be applied to any part of a company's operations up to, and including, full certification. From BS 7750 have stemmed two international environmental management system standards: ISO 14001 and EMAS ISO 14001, respectively.

Producing environmental statements

As outlined above, environmental statements are not compulsory. A company broadly has two choices in relation to how it produces such statements:

- they can be incorporated as part of the annual reports and accounts; or
- they can be stand-alone documents.

Whatever the format of the environmental statements, as with other statements relating to corporate governance issues, companies should be careful to avoid bland statements or statements which simply do not reflect the particular circumstances of the company.

Care should also be taken to reflect the industry within which the company operates and sub-sectors of that industry, depending on the company's lines of business.

Amongst the issues which should be covered in an environmental statement are the following.

- Clear provisions should be made as to environmental-type liabilities. For example, if a company has assets including land which requires remediation (i.e. clean-up costs) due to chemical spillage infiltration or otherwise, this should be clearly stated in the account. The issue becomes, of course, how such assets can be valued. It may well be the case that the remediation costs outweigh the market price of the land even if it were free of contamination. Therefore, signing off in terms of audit and other matters will be particularly crucial in relation to such company assets.

- Such environmental liabilities should take into account current and future cash flows and should also take into account actual and potential litigation costs.

- Environmental obligations, and other costs and expenses, should be noted in the accounts at the first opportunity and not left off the balance sheet until inclusion is deemed appropriate by the company.

- The environmental statement should disclose thoroughly the accounting policies relating to environmental costs and liabilities.

- The statement should also provide background on the company's environmental policy and the programmes it plans to implement in that regard.

- As with other compliance reports, the more thorough, complete and accurate an environmental statement is, the more credibility it will have in the market place and the less opportunity there will be for negative publicity to flow from it.

Environmental trends in corporate governance

The trend has been that, for some years, there has been a growing range of legislation falling under the 'environmental' umbrella. This includes legislation on matters such as waste disposal, contaminated land and land clean-up; product liability; genetic engineering; commercial development of sites, etc. Some of this legislation provides for personal liability on the part of directors and other company officers. It is therefore vital that company directors obtain specific legal advice in relation to their liability.

It may well become the case that many companies establish a sub-committee of the board specifically challenged with dealing with environmental policy and development of environmental risk management techniques for the company. Environmental concern is, and will remain, a focal point of interaction between companies and their many and various stakeholders.

The corporate governance matrix

The inclusion here of comment on the roles of stakeholders in the broad sense is to highlight their growing importance in terms of the corporate governance matrix.

Contemporary corporate governance solutions need to consider the company's position not only from the basis of the shareholders and others within the company but also to keep a 'weather eye' on the external groups and to consider the total context of the company's position.

To keep itself aware of this series of inputs, the board should actively consider the various public relations implications of their intended decisions. This is something we examine in the case studies in Chapter 18.

A diagrammatic depiction of some of the broad parameters of the corporate governance matrix was set out in Chapter 2 (and will be discussed further in Chapter 17). The corporate governance matrix can be represented as in Table 16.1.

The emerging corporate governance matrix in tabular form

We can begin to piece together the key parts of the contemporary and emerging corporate governance matrix, including:

- the key events giving rise to corporate governance;
- the triad of reports;
- the knock-on effect of those reports as they have been adopted by other bodies; and
- the bigger picture inputs affecting the future corporate governance project.

Table 16.1
The emerging corporate governance matrix

Impetus events	Reports	Interested groups	Emerging inputs	Stakeholders
1980s corporate excess and cowboys	Cadbury	London Stock Exchange		Shareholders
1990s recession	Greenbury	Accountancy/law groups, e.g. Accounting Standards Board (ASB)		Customers
Privatisation and boardroom pay	Hampel		Technology revolution, i.e. the Internet	Employees
Move from traditional manufacturing sector			'Mic-Macism' economies Brand-driven companies	Competitors – local and global
Increased environmental awareness			Globalisation	Environmental lobbies
			Media influence	Other models e.g. 'employees first'
			Public relations as crucial	
			Post-modernism	
			The present dominance of the 'shareholders first' model	

We shall explore elements of the emerging corporate governance model in more detail in Chapter 17.

17

UK corporate governance: emerging and future trends

Corporate governance: its changing nature in the 1990s   161

Changing economic models   163

Year 2000 corporate governance   165

Other year 2000 issues   167

Identifying key facets of the UK corporate governance approach   169

Headline corporate governance issues   170

The UK and refining the corporate governance model   170

The emerging corporate governance matrix   171

Corporate governance: its changing nature in the 1990s

As we have seen, corporate governance does not operate in a vacuum but in response to the way in which companies operate and the goals that companies set themselves. Without companies – without the incentive of profit and shareholder return, etc. – there would essentially be no need for corporate governance. A constant theme of the three corporate governance reports and of this book, therefore, is that corporate governance is an adjunct to a company's operations, not a substitute for them.

The wider corporate governance context

Corporate governance developments are an outcome of the domain and operation of companies. Companies, in turn, can only operate in response to a complex array of forces – political, social, economic, cultural, etc. – which operate within a wider context.

Companies therefore operate within a complex matrix of influences and ideas. Obviously, when these forces and ideas shift appreciably in any one direction, there may be a knock-on effect in the way in which companies are operated, governed, or regulated.

Rapid economic and technological change

The 1990s has been characterised as involving episodes of rapid societal change. The intriguing issue is how this rapidity of change, especially of the broad forces at work in society – social, economic, cultural and so on – has a trickle-down effect on corporate governance thinking, and has been reflected in terms of corporate governance practices.

By way of an overview, we will look briefly at the impact of some of the shifts in the so-called 'big forces' that, in turn, have affected the emerging shape of the corporate governance project.

Economic change: The changing nature of the UK and advanced western capital economic systems

Economic systems are now much more interlinked and, as a result, national governments are less able to exert their traditional power. Multinational companies, whose operations spread across many countries, are in effect able to exert power far more quickly and easily than national government. International governmental agencies such as the United Nations are characterised as slow-moving and ineffective. This is because it is a long and complex process to find an accommodation of views and also because such agencies are not run on strictly profit-based lines.

Cultural change: the changing nature of UK and advanced western capital societies, culturally and socially

Cultural theorists have argued that much of the twentieth century has seen the domination of cultural practices, which have emanated from the USA. In fact, one definition of popular culture is that the rest of the world wishes itself to be American. Whilst such an analysis can be overplayed, a strong case can be made for the pervasiveness of the culture emanating from the USA.

There is also a complex relationship between cultural practice and economic practice, in particular, the manner in which companies operate and the atmosphere in which corporate governance operates.

Globalisation

In one sense, globalisation is simply the rapid acceleration of the forces at work outlined above. There is a sense at the moment, certainly in the west, that globalisation is leading to homogenisation of standards. This might, at some stage, translate into some form of European-wide corporate governance mechanism infrastructure. Whilst globalisation emphasises convergence, cultural and economic divergence should not be underestimated. There are deep and powerful forces at play which make cultures, societies and corporate practices in one region of the world quite different from those in another region of the world. A striking instance of this is afforded by examining the sorts of issues that have arisen in the so-called 'Asian crises' of 1997–98.

Technological change

The focal point of any technological change is the Internet. The Internet has surprised even experienced computer industry analysts with the speed and pervasiveness of its influence. Questions abound. How will the Net affect the way in which commerce is undertaken? How will the Net affect the way that companies operate? Will the Net effectively democratise the playing field for start-up businesses? Can a company afford not to have a web page and not to take seriously the concept of e-commerce? And now, of course, there is the looming question of the year 2000 problem (or the millennium bug, as it is known). This is discussed below on page 165.

Changing economic models

Even within the space of the twentieth century and the progress of capitalism, we can identify several broad-banded economic models, and it is within this context of continual change that corporate governance is being mapped.

Within the twentieth century, three broad bands can, and have, been recognised by economists and social theorists:

(a) 'Fordism', i.e. the making of cars, etc. by way of mass-production lines;

(b) 'Sonyism' – mass production still but a changing type of goods, i.e. electric consumables and 'gadgets' including hi-fis etc.;

(c) 'post-Sonyism', where there is a concentration on technology goods; global concentrations. This most advanced of the capital models we might alternatively call the 'mic-mac' model (i.e. Microsoft and McDonald's): they display multinational codes of behaviour; worldwide product and customer bases and applications of management; they are very much brand-led, etc.

There will obviously be overlap between these divisions, i.e. they are not hard and fast. It is interesting, even in the wake of the Internet boom, that Internet providers talk of 'constructing' a web site. The word 'construction' harks back to the Fordist economic era, but has been translated across the divide into the high-tech world of web design and computer functionality.

Economies as 'scientific' systems

Corporate governance can be seen as the naturally occurring part of a mature capitalist economy, i.e. it balances the model of the 'free market' against the 'ethically informed' model.

It recognises that:

(a) there is an ongoing tension, dialogue and debate between the two models;

(b) the ideal business environment lies somewhere on the spectrum between the two extremes;

(c) a market within an advanced capital system cannot be completely 'free', i.e. it isn't a Darwinian jungle where the strong survive and the weak perish;

(d) an approach to ethics as box-ticking and looking over the shoulder should be discouraged;

(e) the corporate governance good practice model is not fixed in stone; it is in the fairly early years of its emergence; over time, the corporate governance model is, and will be, tinkered with, grafted onto and shaped to meet the changing times.

The 1980s boom: blip or natural phenomenon?

Alternatively to viewing the 1980s as some unnatural blip, it may be that the '1980s phenomenon' is a natural event of a maturing 'economy' – almost a scientific phenomenon, an inevitable happening as economies come on-stream: the rampant growth, etc. may be a naturally occurring part of the maturing of an economy; a natural link in the cycle towards maturity.

The 1980s booms were invariably fuelled by the liberalisation of the banking laws and financial regulation systems (witness Big Bang in London in 1986, and the deregulation of Australia's banking laws by a Hawke Labour Government in the early 1980s). Deregulation was a phenomenon that crossed political divides, so that previously tight purse strings were loosened by a flood of incoming money, new international banks and mergers. As a result, the way companies operated altered radically. Businesses grew less through the traditional methods – organic, step-by-step, incremental methods – and, instead, adopted tactics fuelled more by leverage, by larger and larger borrowings. 'Gradualism' was replaced by 'overnightism'.

But it can be seen that the 1980s booms of advanced western economies are finding their parallels a decade later in the Asian so-called economic crisis. Many commentators, and others who have worked there, have testified to a time warp where what has been happening in the 1990s finds a lot of similarity with what went on in the 1980s in the UK and other more advanced economies.

An example of this trend is illustrated in the extract below from an investment banker writing of his recent working experience in Thailand, until recently regarded as one of the emerging tiger economies and now desperately fighting off meltdown.

> The job was turning out to be part accountancy, part private investigator and part showman. In developed economies where corporate governance is stronger and the companies are more mature, there is less scope for abuse.[1]

Corporate governance, then, can be seen as a naturally occurring part of a mature capitalist economy; there is no turning back.

Year 2000 corporate governance

The 'millennium bug'

In the year 2000 a big problem for companies around the world will be how they deal with the anticipated computer bug which experts predict will be triggered when PCs and other computer/software-based equipment attempt to display the date as year 2000.

Companies will need to assess their risk exposure in relation to the anticipated year 2000 problem.

Companies heavily dependent on software and equipment supplies will need to put in place contingency plans. The anticipated problem of the year 2000 will, no doubt, see companies simply producing standard disclosures. If this happens, it will not fit within the evolving corporate governance model, which we have seen elsewhere requires companies to pay particular attention to their own circumstances.

One of the problems with the year 2000 problem is anticipating how extensive it will be. Will it, for example, affect embedded chips (computer hardware within equipment)? Ideally, companies should have a programme in place in order to deal with and overcome any year 2000 problems. The problem is likely to run well beyond issues of the payroll. Manufacturing industries, for example, will have software that deals with a whole array of manufacturing applications and controlled date-dependent devices.

It is certainly likely that the London Stock Exchange will issue fairly onerous reporting requirements in relation to the year 2000 problem. Companies will not be able to rely on the word of their supplies, but will have to test and develop their own contingency plans. Companies will need to carry out 'millennium rollover' tests at their own facilities. They will not simply be able to shift the problem on to consultants, suppliers and others.

For companies, the issue will be what effect the problem has in relation to the share price, both before and after the year 2000 rollover. This, of course, has a direct impact on the board's duties to its stakeholders, including shareholders and employees.

Liability of the board for the year 2000 problem

Company directors and senior executives could face financial ruin from 'millennium bug' litigation because it may well be the case that they are not protected by the usual corporate indemnities. Those indemnities are to the effect that, as long as a director acts within the scope of his employment, and in the best interests of shareholders and employees, who should be financially protected by the company, i.e. if he were to be sued, the company would pay his legal costs in full. The problem with the millennium bug is that it may well be difficult for companies to insure their own directors and officers against damages claims relating to the bug. There is a possibility that a wave of litigation against companies, directors and senior managers who have not adequately prepared for it will follow in the wake of the year 2000 rollover. The only real defence to such a charge will be that companies have implemented a proper and thorough year 2000 programme and that it is in place.

Litigation issues

Potential litigation claims concerning the year 2000 problem include the following:

- claims by investors or creditors who lose money through a lack of disclosure of the year 2000 problem by the company;
- claims by shareholders for a decline in share value because of failure to overcome year 2000 problems;
- actions instituted against companies by regulatory authorities;
- possible class actions against directors and company officers;
- criminal and civil proceedings for breaches of the Companies Act 1985 and other legislation;
- claims for compensation by the company against computer manufacturers, chip manufactures, software producers and others.

Boardroom defences

The defence of 'honest ineptitude' would not be a sufficient excuse to indemnify directors and company officers against year 2000 legal damages. The courts will adopt an objective standard which can be applied to all companies, rather than a 'subjective' standard in which companies could concentrate specifically on their individual circumstances.

Insurance issues

Companies will need to be very careful to ensure that they answer year 2000 questionnaires from their insurers correctly, otherwise the terms of any cover will not encompass the company's circumstances. The trend will be that year 2000 questionnaires become more and more detailed, as insurers look to limit their potential liability to company directors and others.

It is likely that insurers will become tougher and tougher as the year 2000 rollover approaches, and they will refuse to insure directors unless they have completed lengthy and testing questionnaires absolutely accurately. Insurers are already very nervous about the year 2000 problem, and this trend is likely to increase in the course of the 18 months or so before the moment comes.

Smaller companies

The year 2000 problem will be particularly difficult for smaller companies where directors are exposed to company debt by way of personal guarantees.

The problem for smaller companies is that the number of technical staff available for remediation programmes in relation to critical systems will be much harder to find. Larger companies will be able to uphold departments dedicated to compliance procedures.

Obviously, it is difficult to predict the emerging shape of year 2000 corporate governance, but some of the forces which will play a part are outlined below.

Other year 2000 issues

These also include the following factors.

'Globalisation'

The term globalisation, as we saw in Chapter 2, has several strands. It can also be misleading because it may misrepresent the speed of change.

There are divergent forces at work in globalisation. It is not a simple and uncomplicated case of economies 'coming together'. Globalisation can be likened to a weather system: there are turbulences, cross-currents and counter-forces: it represents a complex matrix of influences. An example of the counter-forces can be seen by comparing the 'convergent' forces of globalisation with the divergent forces.

The convergent forces of globalisation

Two of the catchphrase of globalisation are:

(a) 'linkage' – implying more and more interconnectedness of economic systems; and

(b) 'geographic irrelevance', i.e. less regard for traditional state boundaries.

These forces stand for a coming together, a homogenising of economies and conditions. And, while they can be defended and, indeed, built into projects in their own right, at the same time there occur in the globalisation project counterbalancing forces – the divergent forces.

The divergent forces of globalisation

These are what we might label the 'gap phenomenon', in that, at their heart, they illustrate the difficulties of globalisation, the diversity of individual countries and their company structures and outlooks.

It is composed of phenomena, which essentially emphasise the differences, rather than the similarities in economies, in company philosophies, in government philosophies and in cultures.

For examples of divergent forces we could look at:

- environmental attitudes in different parts of the world;
- differing philosophies about the appropriate degree of government involvement in business;
- differing company structures and philosophies, e.g. 'chaebols' in South Korea;
- the degree of 'regulation', as opposed to free market philosophy in, for instance, Japan;
- employee-control company models as, for instance, have been developed in South America.

And, in terms of the EC, the project of convergence meets the irresistible force of divergence in countless episodes so that euphemisms such as 'two-speed' Europe and 'wider' membership (as opposed to 'deeper integration') are deployed to cover the fundamental differences.

Changing economic models

Models of economic behaviour will continue to evolve. Capitalism, for example: will it be a US-style free market, Euro-flavoured or swing towards a Japanese, more interventionist model?

Technology and media power

Shareholder control is likely to broaden from the present narrow base of the AGM as technology enables shareholders to vote and participate more fully in the company's affairs.

Media power is a sign of the times. Companies can harness this power to their ends: to promote ethical transparency of companies; to promote stakeholder-responsible capital and a move away from the 'greed is good' society; and to embrace a notion of profit and enterprise within ethically clear parameters.

Companies need to become more proficient in all aspects of their PR strategy.

Identifying key facets of the UK corporate governance approach

Rebalancing

The Hampel Report makes it clear that the pendulum between business prosperity and accountability has swung too much in favour of accountability in recent years. This is in the light of the succession of three major investigations and reports within the short time-frame (especially in corporate terms) of six years. Without saying as much, Hampel implies that 'corporate governance fatigue' may become a problem with many companies already treating corporate governance compliance as an unnecessary burden to business and adopting a box-ticking attitude to it instead of seeing it as a useful set of tools to assist the prosperity of the business.

Other facets of UK corporate governance

- Growth from now on is likely to be piecemeal and gradualist, and to move away from the major inquiry and report phase.
- Good practice will trickle down to smaller companies.
- Corporate governance benefits will 'cascade' to a wide group of stakeholders.
- The UK model of corporate governance is an internationally influential model.
- Companies are already adapting the model of corporate governance to suit their individual circumstances.

Headline corporate governance issues

Ongoing issues

Ongoing corporate governance issues include:

- directors' pay;
- non-executives' independence;
- bottom line: shareholder returns.

'Weather eye' corporate governance issues

Companies should maintain a watching brief on the following issues:

- moves to formally measure board performance;
- the 10 per cent rule: auditors should not obtain more than 10 per cent of their fees from one company;
- simplifying disclosure rules on executive pay; they have become, according to the Hampel Report, too complex.

Particular issues on the corporate governance horizon

- The year 2000 problem
- Tailoring compliance statements to particular circumstances
- Developing environmental standards and strategies
- Better management of information for key stakeholders, including employees and shareholders
- Creating more effective and more open dialogue with institutional shareholders.

The UK and refining the corporate governance model

The UK, then, has mapped out a comprehensive model. It has achieved a basic blueprint for the balance between the model of the 'free market' and the 'over-regulated' model.

The UK model of governance continues to recognise the following.

Organic growth

The model is not fixed in stone; it is emerging; over time, the model will be tinkered with, grafted on, shaped, sculpted to meet the changing times.

Refinement

The role of business and other parties is to monitor and audit the model.

Consolidation

For the time being, a hands-off and minimalist role is needed; essentially, to let business get on with its job after the period of intense scrutiny afforded by three major corporate governance reports.

The emerging corporate governance matrix

We can begin to piece together the key parts of the contemporary and emerging corporate governance matrix (see Table 17.1), including:

- the key events giving rise to the triad of reports;
- the knock-on effect of those reports as they have been adopted by other bodies; and
- the bigger-picture inputs affecting the future corporate governance project.

Table 17.1
Corporate governance: some of the big picture causes and effects

Inputs	Outcomes
Economies as science systems	Government and banking intervention
Mature economies	Maturing corporate governance models
Directors' liability/litigation costs	Insurance/risk assessment
Economic shocks	Regional and global effects
Post-modernism/popular culture	'Americanisation'
Media technologies revolution	e-commerce
Communication systems revolution	Better information systems
Broadening stakeholder theory (cascading)	Better informed shareholders/ employees
Importance of public relations	Excellent communication required by the board with all the company's stakeholders

Notes

1 Evans, R. (1998) A British banker who rode the tiger, *The Independent on Sunday*, 12 April.

18

Two corporate governance case studies

Overview of the case studies and the approach taken   175

Corporate governance scenarios   176

Case Study 1: Old Tower PLC – boardroom indiscretion   177

Case Study 2: Johnson PLC – directors' pay   184

Overview of the case studies and the approach taken

In this chapter we look at two case studies – practical fact scenarios – which are designed to highlight key corporate governance issues. One way of doing this could have been to take as examples a private limited company, a small public company and a larger listed company. This sort of breakdown, however, would somewhat artificially divide and rule corporate governance issues and not be consistent with the approach taken in the three published corporate governance reports, i.e. the Cadbury, Greenbury and Hampel Reports discussed in this book.

The key facet of the contemporary approach to corporate governance is that it is meant to be changing the 'climate' of business in the UK – the broader ethical, social and economic background – for all companies, irrespective of their size, whilst at the same time allowing them to pursue prosperity for their shareholders.

Whilst the corporate governance focus for compliance has begun with listed companies, there is in place a 'trickle-down' doctrine which sees corporate governance practices as good practice generally, whatever the size, type or shape of company concerned.

To quote the *Code of Best Practice* forming a key part of the Cadbury Report, the first of the corporate governance trilogy of reports published in 1992:

The Code of Best Practice

Introduction, Paragraph 3

The Committee's central recommendation is that the boards of all listed companies registered in the United Kingdom should comply with the Code. The Committee encourages as many other companies as possible to aim at meeting its requirements.

Hence, there is no real advantage to be gained by splitting corporate governance issues on the basis of company size. The corporate governance project will eventually bring all companies under the emerging umbrella of good practice and implement that project step by step and over time, with listed companies leading the way and other companies falling into line.

Corporate governance scenarios

A review of the financial papers in the last 12 months will reveal several corporate governance-related episodes concerning companies. These include company mergers and the issue of employee lay-offs; the independence of non-executive directors; the size of directors' remuneration packages; directors awarding themselves extended contracts; directors awarding themselves compensation payments for reducing their service contracts.

As Gerry Robinson, chairman of Granada, recently said, 'corporate governance is about more than just directors' salaries'. He was responding to shareholder resentment and bad publicity in relation to the fact that, at its recent AGM, Granada proposed the payment of £375 000 in compensation to directors for reducing their service contracts. Some 70 per cent of shareholders supported the payment, but a 30 per cent significant minority opposed the payment. Gerry Robinson said of the episode, 'one of the consequences of the kind of furore we've had over this issue is that you drive people to be dishonest. When contracts are changed, there is always compensation. We could have called it a special bonus or the like, but we've handled it very honestly and straightforwardly and been pilloried for it' (*The Times*, 5 February 1998).

This returns us to one of the themes set out at the beginning of this book, which was: what is meant by the term 'corporate governance'? The Granada episode represents corporate governance in its narrow sense, i.e. the formal system of accountability of senior management to the shareholders. However, it can also be seen that, given the publicity ramifications and the wider stakeholder concern, corporate governance takes into account the more expansive definition which includes 'the entire network of formal and informal relations involving the corporate sector and their consequences for society in general ...'. Corporate governance includes 'the structures, process, cultures and systems that engender the successful operation of the organisations'.[1]

The Granada episode represents the 'underlying problem of corporate governance as recognised by a long tradition of scholars stretching back ... to Adam Smith (1776) ... which lies with the separation of beneficial ownership and executive decision-making in the joint stock company'.[2]

Case Study 1: Old Tower PLC – boardroom indiscretion

Corporate governance issue(s) involved

The 'PR gaffe'; the board's leadership and control roles within the company and in relation to investors and other stakeholders.

Summary position

The directors are indiscreet and cause a nose-dive in the share price, leading to investor dismay and customer anger.

The background facts

Old Tower Football Club PLC has its registered office and 40 000-seat-capacity stadium located in the north-west of England and has been a premiership football club for more than five years. It has not won the premiership in that time, but it has challenged at the top of the Premier League on a couple of occasions and has played in European contests.

Old Tower has been successfully floated on the London Stock Exchange and its shares are trading well. It is not having the best of seasons – its star player out with a serious leg injury, its coach not having recruited heavily and at the same time unfortunately selling the club's number two and three strikers.

The Old Tower crisis

Old Tower has been rocked by intensive media stories appearing in all national newspapers as the result of an undercover 'sting' by a Sunday tabloid, which secretly tape-recorded comments by two key directors of Old Tower criticising the manager, key players and the fan base (especially the females) for, amongst other things, being prepared to pay outrageously inflated prices for Old Tower shirts and other merchandise.

As a result of these stories, the Old Tower share price on the London Stock Exchange has nose-dived, the fans are enraged and are calling for the resignation of the two directors concerned.

The outcome of the Old Tower crisis

After a week of relentlessly bad (and 'getting worse') news stories, the two directors resign, leaving the fans still enraged and the share price down. To make matters worse, the morale at the club sinks as it slips into the relegation zone.

The scenario outlined above is obviously very close to the Newcastle United PLC scenario. It is not without its parallels in terms of other football clubs. They are particularly prone to their own set of issues. These include:

- Timing issues: for example, the timing of the flotation. Should it be at the start of the season, when the team has the possibility of doing particularly well, or some time during the season, or indeed at the end of the season?
- Share price will obviously fluctuate, depending on the fortunes during the season, if they float at the beginning of the season.
- What income will the club receive from television rights, merchandise sales and gate receipts?
- What income will the club receive in terms of transfer fees?
- What costs will the club incur in respect of stadium maintenance and improvement?
- Players' salaries.

As the *Financial Times* commented:

> Aston Villa floated at a bad time. Since June, football shares have come off across the board. But the club also has itself to blame; it floated at a demanding price, and on the pitch its form has been mediocre. But now brokers are upgrading forecasts, with most pitching full-year pre-tax profits at about 8 million pounds. That gives a forward price earning ratio of 15, which looks realistic. However, institutions trying to buy shares yesterday found them hard to come by: this is an illiquid.
>
> Simon Kuper, *Financial Times,* January 1998

The legal angles to the Old Tower crisis

The legal crises facing Old Tower in terms of the case study scenario include:

- director duty and responsibility to the company, generally;
- director responsibility for maintenance of investor confidence and share value;
- director duty to stakeholders, including primarily customers and employees.

The Old Tower corporate governance crisis neatly illustrates the difference between the legal parameters and the corporate governance issues as they apply to directors.

These legal parameters are fairly narrow in some senses and have correspondingly narrow sources – legal cases, legal documents, etc. (See Andrew Sparrow's book on *The Responsibilities of Company Directors* for a full discussion of these matters.)

The corporate governance issues of the Old Tower crisis

The Old Tower scenario highlights the following corporate governance issues.

Leadership

An effective board and its leadership and control role *vis-à-vis* the company are essential. The leadership-control role binds the board collectively and each director individually.

Optimising shareholder returns

The primary beneficiary of corporate governance policy is the shareholders, and this translates into improved share prices and steady dividends. The directors' actions counter this central role of the board and corporate governance policy.

Public reputation

The way in which issues are handled can have a damaging effect on a company's public reputation (Hampel Report, page 18).

Staff/employee resentment

The Greenbury Report highlights the dangers of staff resentment and damage to the company's reputation with respect to poorly handled salary packages to directors. The same considerations apply here.

Negative publicity and the 'new-style' company

Old Tower is a public company; it is also a very high profile company. In fact, football companies and the like are 'top heavy' in this sense – their profiles in terms of media coverage and interest are high in relation to their asset positions and market valuations.

Such 'new-style' companies attract a lot more media attention than do many companies much larger than themselves because what they do, and what they trade in, is popular, readily understood and attracts large TV and newspaper interest. Their core business –

participating in a popular sport (essentially the national sport) – attracts virtually unparalleled interest and media attention.

The directors, then, are in charge of a particularly 'transparent' entity with a 'premium media value', which would put the company well above its FTSE position. There is a 'skewing' between 'size' and 'society fascination'.

A hungry press is always on the lookout for 'human interest' stories concerning such businesses; whether they are to do with the private lives of the players and managers, the reputations of the owners or other angles. In this sense, the directors should be aware that they are in the same firing line of potential press interest.

The directors' performance criteria

What does this mean for the board and each director of such a company?

They must display vigilance, precision and competence.

Vigilance

Vigilance and discretion in terms of their private affairs: who they talk with, who they associate with.

Precision

Precision in their spoken and written communication and what they say and what they write; knowing exactly when to speak off record.

Competence

Utmost competence in their directorial duties. They are in charge of major investment houses, multimillion-pound businesses, which are essentially fairly fragile in that they are vulnerable to 'shocks', e.g. the loss of a key asset – injury to a player; or a 'catastrophic event', e.g. relegation to a lower division.

Board responses

Corporate governance issues

The boards of companies such as Old Tower have to get the corporate governance issues right. They have to comply with the corporate governance recommendations of good practice and they have to be seen to be actively playing the corporate governance game – committed to it as an 'assistance' to their business plans rather than seeing it as a 'business burden' – and consequently dragging their heels in terms of compliance on issues such as:

- boardroom pay;
- remuneration committees;
- the independence of the non-executives on the board; and
- inclusion of well-documented compliance statements and explanations in the annual returns, etc.

PR issues

Because Old Tower is 'punching' well above its weight in terms of its 'market valuation' to 'media fascination' ratios, the board has to play the PR game very well.

It is in a precarious position and the facts related above show how quickly and easily the company's position can change in the light of a PR gaffe by the directors.

The 1990s public company

As was discussed in Chapter 3, the board and each director are in special positions of trust and responsibility to the 'company' which, because it is an artificial entity, essentially translates into the shareholders, the share price and the employees as being key representatives of the company's interests.

Directors are trustees; they are agents; they are themselves employees of the company. Each of these roles involves rigorous ethical demands and high degrees of honesty and trust. They also require a degree of competence.

There is no point in the director relying on a minimal approach to the role – *de minimis*. This would be to the effect, 'I will work to rule; i.e. to the letter of my employment contract and I will do as little as possible.'

The shareholders expect 'exceptional' standards from each director individually, and from the board collectively; they expect from their board 'the best' in the field in terms of direction and strategic planning.

These facets of shareholder demand (rather than mere expectation) include the following.

Unquestionable honesty

The directors will never profit personally from deals made in secret or not disclosed. They act for, and on behalf of, the company and only the company. They do not moonlight for other businesses.

Sustained commitment

A full working week, long hours, weekend commitments, essentially being on call and in company mode seven days a week (to stakeholders, the board is the first, second and third emergency services as far as the company is concerned).

Exceptional competence

In fact, competence becomes an insufficient term; what is needed is a concept of 'total professionalism'.

'Utmost good faith'

The directors have to act in the best interests of the business.

The Old Tower corporate governance dilemma: the company in context

All in all, Old Tower is an example of a company displaying at least a couple of 1990s company phenomena.

Sports company

Old Tower is an example, along with several others, of a sports team being floated successfully on the Stock Exchange, and business seeing it essentially as 'good buy' material in terms of its shares, its business idea and its plans for the future.

A typical asset base

Old Tower is a company whose assets are not typical, traditional business assets such as real property, machines, etc. Old Tower does not fit the traditional economic models that we briefly identified in Chapter 1.

Classifications

Old Tower cannot be described as a 'Fordist' company. Such companies, as we saw earlier, take as their model the manufacturing of a product (cars say), produce them, distribute and sell them to a disparate customer base.

Loyalty factor

Nor can Old Tower be described as 'Sonyist', still essentially product based (though this time more high-tech and personal products in the form of TVs, hi-fis, etc.); its base is football players and customer loyalty. The fans worship the brand through thick and thin, through rain, hail and shine, down motorways, across crowded European skies, those fans will follow the team. They are ideal customers, the model sort of customer, in fact, displaying almost religious devotion to the company, the brand image, the 'product' and all that it stands for.

Possible corporate governance solutions to the Old Tower case

The Old Tower corporate governance solutions include:

(a) rewinding the clock/ensuring that such an incident never happens again;

(b) apologising clearly, completely and quickly and with follow-up remedies which are consistent with the public tone set by the apology;

(c) the directors perhaps being forced to resign if (b) does not work and work quickly;

(d) recognising generally that public relations and corporate governance are very closely linked;

(e) always demonstrating good communication; being clear as to the 'possible' audience that a communication is, or may be, addressed to;

(f) the board and managers needing to be vigilant in optimising shareholder returns and retaining customer loyalty.

Case Study 2: Johnson PLC – directors' pay

This second corporate governance case study involves another issue falling to the remit of the boardroom and that is the issue of pay packages for directors. The Greenbury Report, as we mentioned in Chapters 2, 3 and 4, was specifically set up to deal with this particularly sensitive area of managerial etiquette.

The 'newsworthiness' of lottery-winning-sized packages has not really diminished since the more aggressive media environment engendered in response to them by the early 1990s combination of recession, unemployment, privatisation as new, and the award of, in the public's mind, large and greed-driven salaries. Take, for instance, this report in the business pages of *The Independent* on 18 April 1998:

> £1.8 m for L&G chief
>
> THE CHIEF EXECUTIVE of Legal and General, the insurance group, was awarded a package worth almost £1.8 m in 1997. David Prosser's package included a £1.06 m profit on the sale of share options, a salary of £400,000, a cash bonus of £180,000, and a deferred bonus of £80,000. Total board remuneration, excluding pension contributions and gains on share options, rose 18% to £2.4 m.

This article implicitly criticises the sheer size of such a salary package in a time of tremendous job uncertainty for most people. Take the following extract from *The Independent* on 4 August 1997.

> Financial institutions face a massive shift in employment over the next two years with one hundred and twenty five thousand managers and clerical workers expected to lose their jobs, with the city of London the main beneficiary of a one hundred and thirteen thousand increase in jobs for 'knowledge workers'.

There is a perception that directors will always be able to control the corporate governance environment and the agenda to suit their own interests. That is, they can award themselves 'compensation' for agreeing to reduce the length of their contracts with the company and can justify awarding themselves compensation for agreeing to stay on longer than expected at the company.

There is also a perception that institutional shareholders will generally side with the board in agreeing to such matters at the expense of the small, individual shareholders. In this sense, company boards and institutional shareholders are seen to appear to operate as a kind of 'super economy', which can flout the will of individual shareholders and others.

There have started to be far more widespread reports of shareholder discontent in relation to specific corporate governance issues. For example, the company First Leisure awarded a salary package of more than £4.5 million over the next four years to its chief, Michael Grade, at the same time as proposing to pay £79 000 to a director to extend his contract from one to three years. These sorts of issues had the institutional shareholders seeking clarification and expressing their concern.

Another instance where institutional shareholders and individual shareholders came together was in relation to ousting the entire board of Foreign and Colonial's Brazilian Smaller Companies Investment Trust (Brazit) because of what was perceived as a conflict of interest involving one of its directors who is also a senior figure in the company in which Brazit invested. The shareholders, on a 97 per cent (to 3 per cent) vote, ousted the directors on the principle that the non-executives had not only to be independent but be seen to be independent. The investment trust directors were all meant to be independent non-executives and this was enforced by shareholder say-so.

The corporate governance issue(s) involved in Case Study 2

Directors' salary packages; use of the remuneration committee; boardroom sensitivity, especially to shareholders and employees.

Summary

The appointment of a director and a controversial salary package.

The board not being sufficiently attuned to shareholder concerns.

Background facts

The directors of Johnson Packaging PLC wish to appoint EH, a person highly regarded by some on the board, as marketing director. EH used to work with Johnson Packaging PLC CEO and chairman, Barry Johnson. The proposal is that EH be given a four-year service agreement, which will lock him in on a very high salary package (£300 000 in the first year with possible increments taking it to £600 000 by the start of year 4). There are some unhappy shareholders.

This salary has been set by the board's three-member remuneration committee which is composed of three non-executive directors, only one of whom can be considered independent.

Assume the packaging industry's start-up rate for a marketing director is £120 000 on a rolling one-year contract.

The Johnson Packaging crisis

The shareholders are picketing the company's head office and are planning to go on TV in the next 48 hours.

The outcome of the Johnson case

Johnson relents and drops plans to employ EH. EH is considering taking legal action.

The corporate governance angles and solutions to the Johnson case

The following corporate governance issues and solutions become apparent.

(a) The combining of the role of the CEO and chairman in one-person companies needs careful consideration of particular circumstances and whether this is prudent.

(b) The independence of the non-executives: this becomes especially important in the light of (a).

(c) The use of the remuneration sub-committee on the board: to carefully consider director pay issues and to provide vigorous outside views.

(d) The appointment process. In relation to the appointment of board members:
- directors should be transparent;
- decisions should be taken by the whole board; and
- decisions should be based on the recommendations of a nomination committee (endorsed by both Cadbury and Hampel as 'best practice').

(e) The make-up of the remuneration sub-committee: all three of the non-executives should be independent of the executives.

(f) The length of the proposed service agreement: the Hampel Report strongly recommends, in line with pension fund and insurance groups, that directors should be elected for no more than three years and they should then submit themselves for re-election.

(g) The amount of salary proposed: regard should be seen to be had in broad terms to the prevailing 'market rates' of pay; this is balanced by the broad need to 'recruit, retain and motivate'. Corporate governance is not prescriptive here, but generally expects a balancing of these principles in light of the company's circumstances.

(h) The board's leadership and control role. This involves taking into account, for example:

- the interests of key stakeholders;
- possible employee resentment and staff morale;
- shareholder sensitivity and returns for them; optimising the value-for-money concept;
- broader-issue sensitivity in relation to the share price and company's reputation as 'business-minded'.

General comments

Directors' pay remains a sensitive and pervasive corporate governance issue. In the media (and in the public's mind, apparently), it became and remains artificial to differentiate between privatised companies and companies in general.

It is a sleeping-gun issue. All companies need to be sensitive to perceptions of rewarding themselves over and above notions of fairness. Boards need be sensitive to the possible media angles.

Take the following piece on directors' pay:

> Football union chief gets pay package worth £400,000
>
> GORDON Taylor must be over the moon when he contemplates his pay as chief executive of the Professional Footballers' Association – and the increase he received last year.
>
> Latest figures show that Mr Taylor received a package worth almost £420,000 – nearly 50 per cent up on the previous year, according to the annual report of the official Certification Officer for Trade Unions. His rise was 44 per cent higher than the rate of inflation over most of the year and puts him once more at the top of the league table for union leaders' pay ...
>
> Sick as a parrot, however, must be the general secretaries of more than 100 unions which make returns to the certification officer who get nothing.

> And Mr Taylor's pay ... compares favourably with a number of other union 'barons'. Apart from those who do it for love, a number of others receive a pittance. There is the leader of the Nelson and District Clothworkers and Warehouse Association on £3,479 ....
>
> There are, however, some other 'fat cats' in the union movement ...
>
> Barrie Clement, Labour Editor, *The Independent*, 1 April 1998

Corporate governance solution-based approaches

The Taylor extract usefully illustrates several trends in corporate governance which have been identified, and the need for companies to develop solution-based approaches to their corporate governance strategies.

- The tendency to bundle together corporate governance issues, e.g. pay, industry comparisons, media angles, etc.

- The speed at which corporate governance issues become problems, and problems, in turn, become crises.

- Solutions involve pre-empting the public relations angles, e.g. in the above case, knowing the position in relation to comparable roles.

- Get it right first time and be seen to get it right, i.e. follow transparent guidelines.

- Have properly constituted and thorough-going committees in place.

- Boards maintain a vigilant approach to both the big picture of corporate governance and detailed provisions that trickle down via the recommendations of the corporate governance reports and the changing rules of the Stock Exchange and other bodies.

- Corporate governance, as it is evolving, is not meant to burden business unnecessarily but to balance the chances of 'business prosperity' with 'public accountability'.

- The triad of corporate governance reports – Cadbury, Greenbury and Hampel, creates a sliding scale of compliance from 'compulsory' or 'strongly recommended' compliance at one extreme to low-level compliance at the other. The practical effect of these reports is essentially to put in place a set of clear and workable benchmarks with which business can work in both the short and long term.

- Corporate governance is, and seems set to remain, essentially about 'good communication' by companies in the fullest sense of the term with their range of stakeholders.

Notes

1 Keasey, K. and Wright, M. (1997) 'Issues in corporate accountability and governance', *Accounting and Business Research*, 19A, 291–303.

2 Keasey, K., Thompson, S. and Wright, M. (eds) (1997) *Corporate Governance, Economic Management and Financial Issues*, Oxford: Oxford University Press.

Glossary of terms

Box-ticking

Treating corporate governance as a compulsory code rather than as a useful assistance to business; the board seeing it as merely ticking off the requirements 'mechanically' rather than adapting the scheme to meet the company's own concerns where possible.

Best Practice, Code of

See Cadbury.

Cadbury

Sir Adrian; Chair of the Cadbury Report and *Code of Best Practice*, 1992;
see Chapter 3.

Code of Best Practice

See Cadbury.

Directors' duties

Encompass fiduciary duties (i.e. duties of trust and honesty), and negligence (i.e. competence in the job and the quality of decision making).

Ethics

An alternative way of saying 'corporate governance' when applied to companies; embraces the notions of how and why a company goes about its functions as well the narrower question of what the company does; see Chapters 2 and 9.

Executive director

A full-time director
see 'non-executive' and Chapters 4 and 5.

Fordism

A reference to shop-floor mechanisation, i.e. the first wave of mass-producing factories producing cars etc.; gave way to Sonyism (or post-Fordism);
see Chapters 2 and 17.

Garden leave

Where a senior employee, typically a director, is paid to stay away from the business during the period of notice between setting the departure date from the company and the date itself, e.g. 3 months or 6 months. During this time the executive gets the chance literally to cut the lawn and the company ensures that confidential information, customer lists and goodwill generally are kept intact. See Chapter 4.

Globalisation

The phenomenon particularly apparent in the 1990s of the increasing interlinking of economic systems; see Chapters 2 and 17.

Golden handcuff

An incentive package for a senior executive to stay as opposed to a golden handshake (see Chapter 4).

Golden handshake

A payment over and above the service agreement entitlement on a senior executive's departure (see Chapter 4).

Goodwill

An intangible business asset similar to reputation; will suffer if corporate governance problems are perceived.

Greenbury

Sir Richard; Chair of the second corporate governance report published in 1995 and focusing on executive pay.

Hampel

Sir Ronnie; Chair of the third corporate governance report published in January 1998.

Mass media

A product of the mechanisation of society characterised by Fordism; relevant in terms of 1990s corporate governance by virtue of the growing importance of 'PR outcomes' for companies, especially sensitive decisions taken by the board such as director pay levels; see Chapters 2 and 17 and the case studies in Chapter 18.

Mic-Macism

A reference to the current technology revolution, which has seen an explosion in the use of home computers, software, CD roms and now the Internet as computers begin to talk to one another through e-mail, etc.

'Mic' refers to Microsoft; 'Mac' refers to McDonald's; both are global corporations with strong codes of conduct; both are key players in terms of global culture and capital values.

Models of corporate governance

We can identify three possible models:

(a) 'hassle' or over-regulation; this encourages a box-ticking approach to corporate governance (See 'box-ticking') and mistakenly promotes corporate governance into an end and not a means.

(b) minimal, i.e. a *de minimis* approach where there are few if any controls on a company's ethical performance.

(c) value-added and balanced, i.e. due weight is given to the competing interests of 'business prosperity' and 'public accountability' (this is the purported UK model).
See Chapters 2, 3 and 17.

Non-executive director

A part-time director.
May be independent of the executive or not.
See 'executive' and Chapter 4.
Their independence forms an important link in corporate governance compliance, for example in relation to the remuneration sub-committee for directors.
See 'sub-committee'.

Public relations (PR)

The Institute of Public Relations defines PR as 'the deliberate, planned and sustained effort to establish and maintain mutual understanding between an organisation and its publics'.

Restraint of trade (ROT)

Restraining a senior employee in relation to their employment business opportunities after they have left the company. ROT clauses are found in service agreements and to stand up in court must be commercially reasonable. They will typically include a time, distance and type of business restriction, e.g. Employee X for 12 months and within 10 miles cannot work or set up a Y-type business.
See Chapter 15.

Shareholder

Same as 'member'.
The key target of UK corporate governance compliance.

Shareholder models

Refers to shareholders' working relationship with the board:

(a) *de minimis*

(b) occasional, i.e. AGM based

(c) hands-on.

The Hampel Report recommends improving the quality of the AGM 'experience' for shareholders through more effective board communication.
See Chapter 14.

Sonyism

A reference to the production of typically household-entertainment goods, e.g. TVs, hi-fis, and so on; succeeded Fordism and is currently being succeeded by 'Mic-Macism', see Chapters 2 and 17.

Stakeholder

Those interested in the company's performance and its corporate governance compliance: principally the shareholders, second, the employees, third, others such as creditors. This broad view of stakeholding is endorsed by the Hampel Report.
See Chapters 2 and 4.

Sub-committees

Three are identified for corporate governance purposes:
- appointment to the board;
- remuneration of directors; and
- audit and overseeing the board's relationship with the auditor.

See 'non-executive directors'.

Ten per cent rule

Refers to the recommendation that the company should not supply more than 10 per cent of an auditor's fee base; to exceed it would put the auditor's independence in jeopardy.

See Chapter 9.

Bibliography

Cadbury, Sir A. (1992)

The Cadbury Report:

(a) *The Code of Best Practice*

(b) *The Financial Aspects of Corporate Governance*

London: Gee Publishing.

Clarke, A. (1996)

Business Entities: A practical guide

London: Sweet and Maxwell.

ISBN 0 421 50490 0

Derwent R. A. and Jones, M. E. (eds) (1997)

The Corporate Governance Handbook

London: Gee Publishing.

Greenbury, Sir R. (1995)

The Greenbury Report *Directors' Remuneration*

London: Gee Publishing.

ISBN 1 86089 012 1

Griseri, P. and Groucutt, J. (1997)

In Search of Business Ethics

London: Financial Times, Pearson Professional Ltd.

ISBN 0 273 63204 3

Guidelines for Directors (1995)

London: IOD (reprinted 1997)

ISBN 0901 230 480

Hampel, Sir R. (1998)

The Hampel Report *Committee on Corporate Governance: Final Report*

January 1998

London: Gee Publishing.

ISBN 1 86089 034 2

Keasey, K., Thompson, S. and Wright, M. (eds) (1997)
Corporate Governance: Economic, management and financial issues
Oxford: Oxford University Press.
ISBN 0 19 828 991 X

Keasey, K. and Wright, M. (eds) (1997)
Corporate Governance: Responsibilities, Risks and Remuneration
Chichester: John Wiley.

Novak, M. (1997)
On Corporate Governance: The corporation as it ought to be
Washington DC: The AEI Press.
ISBN 0 8447 7082 5

Sparrow, A. (1998)
The Responsibilities of Company Directors (second edition)
London: Financial Times Managment Briefings.
ISBN 0 273 63780 0

Tricker, R. (1996)
Pocket Director: The essentials of corporate governance from A to Z
London: The Economist Books.
ISBN 1 86187 000 5

Vidal, J. (1997)
McLibel: Burger Culture on Trial
London: Macmillan.
ISBN 0 330 35237 7

Warner, J. (1998)
'Stakeholding gone mad, or is this the future?'
The Independent, 18 April.